THE STEADFAST LEADER

THE STEADFAST LEADER

Control Anxiety, Make Confident
Decisions, and Focus Your Team Using the
New Science of Leadership

RANDY BRAZIE, MD, SEP

GEOFFREY VANDERPAL, DBA, CFP®

New York Chicago San Francisco Athens London Madrid
Mexico City Milan New Delhi Singapore Sydney Toronto

1 2 3 4 5 6 7 8 9   LCR   28 27 26 25 24 23

ISBN   978-1-265-52448-7
MHID   1-265-52448-3

e-ISBN   978-1-265-52551-4
e-MHID   1-265-52551-X

Library of Congress Cataloging-in-Publication Data

Names: Brazie, Randy, author. | Vanderpal, Geoffrey, author.
Title: The steadfast leader : control anxiety, make confident decisions, and
    focus your team using the new science of leadership / Randy Brazie,
    MD, SEP & Geoffrey Vanderpal, DBA, MBA, CFP, CLU, CTP, PMP,
    SHRM-CP/SCP, CSCP ; foreword by Deb Dana, LCSW.
Description: New York : McGraw Hill, [2023] | Includes bibliographical
    references and index.
Identifiers: LCCN 2023033653 (print) | LCCN 2023033654 (ebook) |
    ISBN 9781265524487 (hardback) | ISBN 9781265525514 (ebook)
Subjects: LCSH: Leadership. | Leadership—Psychological aspects. |
    Decision making. | Executive ability.
Classification: LCC HD57.7 .B7338 2023 (print) | LCC HD57.7 (ebook) |
    DDC 658.4/092—dc23/eng/20230726
LC record available at https://lccn.loc.gov/2023033653
LC ebook record available at https://lccn.loc.gov/2023033654

McGraw Hill books are available at special quantity discounts to use as premiums and sales promotions or for use in corporate training programs. To contact a representative, please visit the Contact Us pages at www.mhprofessional.com.

McGraw Hill is committed to making our products accessible to all learners. To learn more about the available support and accommodations we offer, please contact us at accessibility@mheducation.com. We also participate in the Access Text Network (www.accesstext.org), and ATN members may submit requests through ATN.

CONTENTS

FOREWORD
BY DEB DANA, LCSW

The autonomic nervous system is at the heart of daily life. What begins with our biology shapes the way we live, love, and work. It is the neural platform beneath every experience. And yet, most of us have no idea how this system works or how to work with it. With the development of Polyvagal Theory, Stephen Porges provided a modern map of the territory of the autonomic nervous system and a new understanding of the ways it shapes moment-to-moment experiences of connection and protection.

As a clinician with a specialty working with complex trauma, I love neuroscience and have always brought an understanding of the brain to my clinical work. When I discovered Polyvagal Theory, I added what had been a missing piece of the puzzle to my understanding of client symptoms and suffering. I became intrigued with integrating a polyvagal perspective into my therapy sessions to help my clients learn to become active operators of their nervous systems and navigate their lives with a sense of regulation and safety. As I developed a polyvagal approach to clinical work, it became clear that the nervous system was an integral part of the therapy

process no matter what modality was being utilized—
that in every session a therapist was engaging with their
client's nervous system. In order to introduce a polyvagal
perspective, I had to learn to speak the language of the
nervous system and create a structure for therapists and
clients to engage in nervous system to nervous system
communication. Out of necessity, I became a polyvagal
translator.

After years of developing ways to integrate science
and psychotherapy, I've begun to explore ways to bring
Polyvagal Theory to the population I call curious human
beings. Polyvagal Theory has a universal appeal in that it
is not a clinical protocol. It is the science of how we are
human and can be applied to every aspect of daily living.
Since the nervous system is a common denominator in
our human experience, learning how this system works
leads to understanding ourselves and others in a new
way. When we apply the principles of Polyvagal Theory,
we can become active operators of our nervous systems,
find regulation in everyday moments, and more skillfully
meet the larger challenges that are present in our lives.

The times we live in call for this level of understanding. There is an imperative to change the familiar
paradigm that preferences brain over body and disregards
the impact physiology has on our ability to communicate, collaborate, manage stress, and meet the challenges
of the work environment. In *The Steadfast Leader*, Randy
Brazie and Geoffrey VanderPal brilliantly answer that
call using their individual areas of professional expertise
to integrate neuroscience and business and transform the
way we think about leaders and leadership.

The Steadfast Leader relies on the principles of Polyvagal Theory to define the qualities of a good leader and

create the foundation for developing successful teams, finding financial success, and navigating the challenges of today's workplace. Brazie and VanderPal introduce the concept of instinctive leadership and illustrate how integrative thinking—using both brain power and body wisdom—impacts organizational experience and business outcomes. Throughout the book they stay true to their mission of bringing the worlds of neuroscience and business together, keeping a focus on understanding the impact of environmental and interpersonal cues of danger and safety in the workplace and the consequences of autonomic state shifts to team building, productivity, and the decision-making process.

Oliver Green, the fictitious executive introduced in Chapter 1 and then followed throughout the book, is an easy-to-relate-to figure whose journey illustrates the role of biology in determining how someone leads and examines the path to leadership through the lens of the nervous system. Each professional scenario demonstrates the ways changes in biology directly impact style of leadership, integrative thinking, and either interrupt or resource the creation of a sense of safety for leaders themselves and for their teams that is essential for success.

The Steadfast Leader is a beautiful collaboration between two old friends, both experts in their fields, that presents a convincing argument for incorporating a polyvagal perspective into the world of work and fundamentally changes the landscape of how we think about the qualities of successful leaders and good leadership.

INTRODUCTION

What drives leadership, management, and financial practices in today's business culture? The global community wants to know. Since you're reading this book, this is also a topic of interest for you. Yes, researchers have their theories and offer considerable insights into the intellectual and psychological factors that contribute to success or failure, but these theories are seldom fully applicable in real life. Researchers aren't at ground level experiencing the myriad challenges leaders and employees face in the workplace every day. What's more, daily challenges can exacerbate existing stress and trauma, which can negatively impact decision-making. This puts the success of the business, the leader, and the employee at risk. An instinctive leader knows how to avoid this bleak scenario.

In *The Steadfast Leader*, we introduce you to the concept of *instinctive leadership*, not another leadership style but rather a quality of excellent leadership, and how to strengthen this skill to improve resilience toward work stressors for everyone in the workplace. Drawing from the latest scientific research and applying it to the real world, we strengthen the topical theories and models and delve into them to reach what's really at the core but so often overlooked. By emphasizing the *instinctive* cognitive dimension of decision-making, we fill in the missing piece of the puzzle needed to achieve success in a variety of professional landscapes.

The idea for this work was conceived during a dinner conversation, many of which we have had over the course of our longtime friendship. On this occasion, we discussed the bridge between our fields of study, which led to a collaboration on several articles and ultimately to this book. Drawing from and combining our knowledge in the fields of psychiatry (Randy) and business/finance (Geoffrey), we explore the interface between neuroscience and the business world and present our findings and insights throughout this book.

In Chapter 1, we explain the origins and components of the Polyvagal Theory (simply, how the state of our autonomic nervous system impacts our thoughts and behavior) in relation to instinctive leadership. This leadership skill requires leaders to understand how to unlock the full potential of their cognitive *and* somatic mental faculties to improve their professional outcomes. We discuss the three descending states of the autonomic nervous system—socialization and safety, mobilization, and immobilization—from the perspective of the "Polyvagal Ladder," coined by clinician and consultant Deb Dana, who so graciously wrote the Foreword to this book. To put this into context, we explore the conditions that can compel a worker to shift between the three autonomic states and the resulting consequences.

In Chapter 2, we narrow down the real-life applications of instinctive leadership and the Polyvagal Theory in modern organizations. Considering the rapid evolution of technology and business systems, it is essential for leaders to compare the strengths and weakness of popular and emerging leadership styles. Therefore, we focus on four common leadership approaches: transactional, transformational, servant, and situational leadership. We discuss how the Polyvagal Theory can be integrated into these leadership styles to improve the outcomes of rational (analytical) and nonrational (intuitive and evaluative) decision-making.

In Chapter 3, we answer the all-important question, "How can leaders achieve success in terms of human resource management?" Most organizations sensibly place much emphasis on talent acquisition, requiring leaders to have an in-depth understanding of recruitment and selection processes. However, depending on the recruitment staff's perspective and autonomic state, specific types of bias and discrimination often emerge during recruitment and selection. With that in mind, we offer suitable recommendations for creating a solid workforce and eliminating prejudice in the talent acquisition process.

Using the example of the financial sector to underscore the importance of combining rational and nonrational decision-making, in Chapter 4, we focus on the main prerequisites for financial success in the modern business environment. We also outline several types of bias and discrimination that prevent leaders from making optimal financial decisions in their respective fields. We emphasize the roles of intelligence, emotions, and instinct in financial decision-making with the overall objective of illustrating how the business leader can combine multiple dimensions of their mental faculties to achieve goals.

Our focus in Chapter 5 turns to the physiological qualities and personal attributes that define good teams. To illuminate how the Polyvagal Theory and instinctive leadership correlate with good teamwork, we stress the importance of the three autonomic states with regard to conflict and conflict resolution from the perspective of both leadership and staff. This approach highlights traits and skills that team leaders and members must cultivate to optimize the team's productivity. We also offer several recommendations for strengthening team performance.

While the previous chapters focus largely on the leader's viewpoint, in Chapter 6, we consider the perspective of employees in successful leadership. Although leaders may attempt unique strategies for improving leadership outcomes, certain situations arise in which employees lack the necessary motivation to support their leaders. In such cases, leaders need to develop an in-depth understanding of their workers' intrinsic and extrinsic needs in relation to their job characteristics. Therefore, we narrow down several evidence-based measures that can improve employee motivation, retention, and overall satisfaction levels.

In Chapter 7, we reveal the secrets leaders need to know to strengthen both their rational and nonrational mental faculties. We drive home the importance of nurturing intuitive intelligence in the modern professional environment. Given that there is no one-size-fits-all strategy in leadership, we encourage business managers and leaders to use innovative strategies to maintain an optimal cognitive state. In business, conflicts are virtually unavoidable, so we also provide the steps leaders need to follow toward resolution. Leaders will learn how to combine logical and instinctive decision-making in both calm and high-pressure environments.

The book's conclusion summarizes all the factors that make a leader an *instinctive* leader—one whose strategy incorporates integrated decision-making in all facets of the professional landscape. It blends together the insights offered throughout the book into a usable takeaway description of instinctive leadership.

To bring all these concepts to life, we provide an ongoing professional scenario based on a fictitious young executive named Oliver Green, a thread we weave throughout all the chapters. This executive, of course, could be any age, gender, race, or nationality working in virtually any industry. Rather than try to cover all our bases and muddy the playing field, we follow Oliver specifically so that you can see how the concepts build upon one another and play out in different situations and circumstances. Although the spotlight is on Oliver, think of him as everyman or everywoman and apply his experiences to your own leadership approach and challenges.

Our main objective with this book is to illustrate how modern professionals respond to different stimuli in their respective environments to build a structured plan to nurture skills and competencies that allow everyone in the organization, but especially leaders, to make optimal decisions regardless of their physiological states. By turning off or mitigating defensive responses, workers can merge rational and nonrational decision-making in their daily practices. In addition to cultivating instinctive leadership, both leaders and employees will learn how to turn on their social engagement system during times of distress. This competency is vital for business leaders who handle complex scenarios on a frequent basis.

The exploration of the factors that influence organizational decision-making reveals that staff performance and productivity are dependent on the characteristics of their surrounding environment and the people within these surroundings. Thus, the principal goal of understanding the Polyvagal Theory as it relates to instinctive leadership is to elaborate on how to identify and overcome fear and stress in the workplace and create a conducive work environment for achieving success. It is our intention to provide you with the information necessary to create a steadfast foundation from which to launch yourself and your team to ever greater heights.

CHAPTER 1

Why Leaders Should Care About the Polyvagal Theory

What are the elements that shape good professionals and business leaders? Some believe that good leaders are born, while others embrace the belief that good leaders are nurtured by instilling adequate knowledge, skills, and experience. Although significant research has been performed to support these ideas in the modern business environment, the reality is that the studies are based on standard assumptions about human decision-making. The inherent focus on rational, or analytical, decision-making often conceals the fact that the professional environment is complicated and that this type of decision-making is often limited or impractical. Senior and junior workers must learn to maneuver through their personal and professional challenges both at work and at home. Considering that even the most senior worker is still a human being, these challenges can accumulate and begin to influence their decisions at work. Understanding the Polyvagal Theory and how it applies to the business world is the first step toward demystifying the rational (analytical) and nonrational (intuitive and evaluative) factors that affect professional decisions in different environments. Let's begin.

What Is the Polyvagal Theory?

The Polyvagal Theory is a concept that was developed in the 1990s by world-renowned researcher Stephen Porges, PhD, that explains our instinctive response to seek a sense of safety and/or connection with others in different circumstances, situations, and environments. We'll delve more deeply into the science and history behind the theory itself later, but for now, it's just important to acknowledge that in a typical environment, we human beings follow our daily routines and make decisions that do not require too much thought. Even the most challenging task can be accomplished if we understand how to resolve it. However, the Polyvagal Theory stresses that we also face uncommon scenarios that may force us to make on-the-spot decisions, such as whether to plow through, escape, or do nothing.

Myriad situations can pull us from our comfort zones, leading to uncomfortable states such as fear, stress, and trauma, which shake our mental and emotional well-being enough to result in decisions that are not based on logic or forethought. In situations that cause the fight-or-flight response, the subconscious overrides the thinking brain in a process that's often referred to as "amygdala hijack." The amygdala, by the way, is the part of the brain responsible for emotions and memories. When the thinking brain is relegated to the passenger seat, logic and reason (and, presumably, good decision-making) are out of reach.

The Polyvagal Theory looks at the neurobiological mechanisms behind these behaviors and offers guidance on how to improve decision-making in the face of such challenges. While cognitive psychology concepts and models can explain most areas of leadership, business, and financial behaviors, human psychology has more primitive elements that have not been adequately explored within the modern business environment. Nevertheless, they are equally powerful and influential. The Polyvagal Theory can explain the underlying influences that are not fully addressed by cognitive psychology in modern-day leadership, human resource management, and financial disciplines. To illustrate this, let us introduce you to Oliver Green and see what happens when his overreliance on rational decision-making results in decreased productivity in his new leadership role.

Putting the Spotlight on Senior Executive Oliver Green

Oliver Green is the youngest senior executive in a stock trading firm, where he has worked for 10 years. The company has been recording significant growth, and Oliver feels he's played a vital role in the organization's recent successes. He has established a formidable reputation for being an analytical thinker who understands when to cut losses or to continue to support the investment until it realizes consistent profits. One of his newer responsibilities as a result of his recent promotion includes recruiting new talent and supervising them during their first years of tenure. He is also in charge of handling interactions with major shareholders and resolving employee disputes. No amount of analysis can help him with these "wild card" responsibilities.

While Oliver enjoys making investment decisions, he often feels overwhelmed participating in the recruitment of workers and the supervision of employees. Although other senior executives perform similar roles, they have decades of accumulated knowledge and experience and seem to easily make instinctive decisions when they lack adequate information. Oliver is stressed and feels that his responsibilities are draining him; he no longer finds satisfaction performing even the roles that had previously excited him. Whenever he is faced with a major decision, he feels disoriented. Sometimes he freezes up, uncertain whether his decision will have a positive or negative effect. Recently, he was forced to release five employees due to restructuring, a matter he found unpalatable and stressful.

The accumulation of these issues has been affecting not only his overall outlook but also his investment choices. In his own words, he's been experiencing an "unlucky streak." Aware of his decline in productivity, Oliver sought advice from some of the more experienced senior executives, which included statements like "Just copy how we handle these activities," "It's bad luck—you'll get past it," "Take a vacation; this job can be very stressful," and "A few courses on leadership and human resource management will help." Although these responses were relatively useful, they were not immediate solutions to Oliver's problems. After persisting, he finally got some advice that resonated with him: "Learn to be aware and to respect your gut."

This response encouraged Oliver to question how he usually makes decisions. In most cases, he makes good decisions when he has enough time and knowledge to analyze his options. However, there are many situations where he is forced to make decisions without adequate information. In those cases, analyses are useless. He thinks perhaps he should start relying on his instincts as well. But how would he go about nurturing useful instinctive decision-making?

Can you see from Oliver's case that both rational and nonrational decision-making are vital to successfully hold a leadership position in the modern professional environment? Failure to resolve the conflict between the two decision-making approaches can cause a decline in performance and productivity. Nonrational thinking, which involves intuition and evaluation, is an important aspect of decision-making, but it is not cultivated in the modern professional environment. In his typical state, Oliver has shown that he can make good decisions. However, when he is in the sympathetic (fight-or-flight) state as a result of accumulated stress, his decisions are adversely affected by negative psychological influences. He needs to learn how to return to a state of balance, where rational and nonrational decision-making can best guide his choices—and that's where the Polyvagal Theory can shed some light on how nervous system state shifts bias perspective.

The Components of the Polyvagal Theory

Stephen Porges published "The Polyvagal Theory: New Insights into Adaptive Reactions of the Autonomic Nervous System" in 1995. In a follow-up article in 2009, he summarized several features of the theory including that the autonomic nervous system regulates involuntary physiologic processes such as heart rate, blood pressure, respiration, and digestion. According to the article, "The polyvagal theory proposes that the evolution of the mammalian autonomic nervous system provides the neurophysiological substrates for adaptive behavioral strategies. It further proposes that physiological state limits the range of behavior and psychological experience."[1]

What this means in plain English is that we have the inherent ability to develop strategies that allow us to adapt to and respond to our environment but also that what's going in our bodies at any given time in response to stimuli affects our emotions, thoughts, and actions, giving us a more limited perspective. The article further states, "The theory links the evolution of the autonomic nervous system to affective experience, emotional expression, facial gestures, vocal communication, and contingent social behavior,"[2] highlighting that social interactions are an important consideration in stable environments as well as when a person faces external threats.

So, what determines our response to stimuli in general? It's the interplay of the three subsystems of our autonomic nervous system (see Figure 1.1):

1. Ventral vagal complex
2. Sympathetic nervous system
3. Dorsal vagal complex

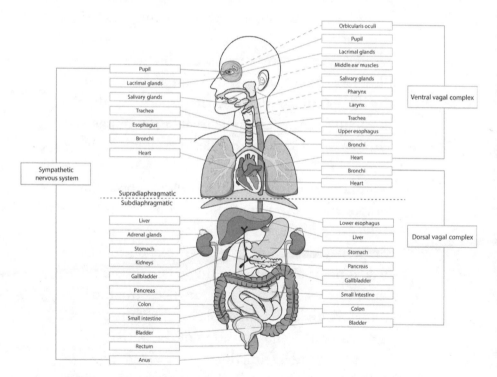

Figure 1.1 The Three Subsystems of the Autonomic Nervous System

Source: Kolacz, J., Kovacic, K.K., & Porges, S.W. (2019). Traumatic stress and the autonomic brain-gut connection in development: Polyvagal Theory as an integrative framework for psychosocial and gastrointestinal pathology, *Developmental Psychobiology 61*(5), 3.

The three components of the autonomic nervous system focus on different cognitive functions. Let's take a closer look at each:

- **Ventral vagal complex (VVC).** Foremost, the ventral vagal complex (VVC) is oriented toward understanding the mechanisms of social engagement. The VVC usually supports the neural processes that involve prosocial behaviors and social connections. Sullivan et al. claimed that the VVC regulates and controls facial, head, and ear muscles, thereby allowing for coordinated communication, listening, and listening ability.[3] For that reason, this subsystem of the autonomic nervous system determines social interactions and allows a person to decide how to resolve social challenges. In a business setting, the VVC allows us to determine and handle social interactions with our superiors, work colleagues, and subordinates.

- **Sympathetic nervous system (SNS).** The second component of the autonomic nervous system is the sympathetic nervous system (SNS). This component determines a person's response to an evaluation of their surrounding environment to determine whether to "fight" or "flee." In other words, the SNS is responsible for the fight-or-flight response. The activation of the SNS can increase metabolic functions to the extent of mobilizing the human body to perform evasive actions.[4] Other functions include increased heart rate, tensed muscles, and the release of hormones that mobilize the human body to seek safety or survival. Overall, the SNS can affect cognitive functions by altering behaviors to evaluate the environment and determine how one should respond to adverse events. The SNS is responsible for helping us determine how to respond when facing negative emotions or psychological influences.

- **Dorsal vagal complex (DVC).** The final component is the dorsal vagal complex (DVC). While the SNS focuses on evaluating the surrounding environment for danger, the DVC controls the neural and muscle systems to react to danger, terror, or extreme stress. Reliable research studies reveal that the DVC places the human body in a passive state, which allows it to reserve metabolic resources and reduce oxygen demands in order to ensure survival.[5] However, these activities can also cause the human body to freeze or "shut down" in response to stress. In Oliver Green's case, the DVC was responsible for his disorientation and tendency to freeze when faced with making major organizational decisions.

In summary, the VVC is oriented toward supporting social engagement in an environment that is perceived as safe, whereas the SNS and DVC tend to induce mobilization or immobilization, respectively. It's important to mention here that there are different intensity levels of each state. While all three components serve vital purposes in human life, in this book, much of our focus is on the *negative* aspects of the mobilization state (fight-or-flight, specifically) and the immobilization state in the workplace and the potential consequences of those states.

Obviously, some mobilization is required for everyday functions, including the positive experience of play and collaboration.

Let's look at the implications of this information in the scenario for our executive Oliver Greene:

Unlocking the Potential of Somatic Psychology

Oliver Green underwent significant training to become an efficient decision maker, which accounts for his rapid promotion to senior executive. However, there are many instances where his theoretical knowledge fails to return the expected results. For instance, Oliver is familiar with various leadership strategies, but some of those are impractical in intense organizational situations. For instance, during times of conflict, Oliver tends to avoid dealing with the situation. Freezing up is a realistic reaction to stress and fear, but it can also be perceived as a sign of weakness. Therefore, Oliver's main challenge involves his inability to unlock the full potential of somatic psychology, which emphasizes how one's physical and emotional state influences the mind and how to adapt to this state.

Although most organizational scenarios require rational thinking, the value of somatic psychology in building instinctive leadership skills cannot be overstated. With this knowledge, Oliver will gain the ability to strengthen rational decision-making with somatic thinking—that is, nonrational decision-making.

If you're wondering how these somatic systems are related to leadership and the professional environment, place your focus on the decision-making functions of these systems. Research shows that these systems play an important role not only in controlling people's physiological responses but also in how people make decisions when faced with various challenges.[6] Constructs such as fear, anger, and stress can compel a person to subconsciously transition across the different states. Although these states may not manifest physically, they tend to emerge in the person's behavior, including decision-making. So, given that the human physiological state can be forcefully shifted from the steady state to the extreme state in the face of changing circumstances, the Polyvagal Theory can help business leaders learn to consciously recognize when this shift occurs, return to the more neutral state, and then make use of both rational and nonrational cognitive mechanisms to drive toward success.

In modern society, neuroscience has become a vital resource for explaining the factors that drive human actions and behaviors. The information has been used to develop strategies for improving the functional outcomes of the human brain. The most well-known theory of neuroscience involves the classification of the brain according to different hemispheres that control reading, writing, speaking, communication, counting, creativity, language, comprehension, and nonverbal skills.[7] In this context, the area of the brain that controls rational decision-making is the prefrontal cortex (the thinking brain), whereas nonrational functions such as emotions are determined by the limbic system, which is involved in emotional learning and memory as well as detection of danger versus safety. To clarify, the autonomic nervous system is triggered directly by input from the limbic system. If the limbic system decides there is danger (even if no *true* danger is present), it sends signals to the prefrontal cortex, compelling the prefrontal cortex to respond by making a decision whether to fight or flee. When a life-or-death response isn't necessary, the thinking brain needs somatic input to calm down, which can be achieved with the techniques we'll introduce later in the book.

The Psychology Behind Instinctive Decision-Making

Oliver Green aims to become a leader that his subordinates and supervisors respect. Even though his journey may be long and tiresome, he is determined to prove his value as an essential member of the organization. Oliver's greatest asset is his familiarity with organizational and human resource concepts. However, this knowledge is insufficient for guiding his department. From his perspective, the best approach is to nurture instinctive leadership to exploit the full potential of his rational and nonrational faculties. With that in place, decisions that require rational decision-making will be solved through logical, analytical approaches. However, choices that require emotional variables will be addressed with a more appropriate strategy. Accordingly, the understanding of instinctive leadership is essential to allow Oliver to take advantage of both his rational and nonrational faculties. This approach will make him an effective leader who can make the best choices for his employees and the entire company.

Somatic Psychology Versus Cognitive Psychology

The Polyvagal Theory informs the field of somatic psychology, a body-oriented approach to psychology, rather than from traditional cognitive psychology, which focuses on how people think. In recent years, rational decision-making has been highlighted as one of the most important competencies of successful professionals. These researchers have focused on the "thinking brain" as the main prerequisite for a person's success. Research describes rationality as "an analytic, systematic, rule-based, and explicit mechanism for decision-making."[8] These types of professionals follow step-by-step decision-making practices. However, this approach is usually ideal in the perfect scenario where the person has adequate time, knowledge, and resources to perform accurate evaluations. Therefore, rationality is often based on hypothetical scenarios that describe the professional environment as a space where workers follow specific rules and standards.

In reality, human beings do not always adhere to the standards. As shown in Oliver Green's case, leaders are often forced to make quick decisions with limited time. In such scenarios, those who rely on rational decision-making will be more likely to fail than those who can make instinctive decisions with what information they have. Researchers who focus only on the "thinking brain" often miss half the puzzle when they try to explain decision-making in the modern business environment. Nonrationality, or intuition, which is a component of instinctive thinking, is an important decision-making quality that can allow modern professionals to overcome the slow and time-consuming characteristics of rational thinking.[9]

The Difference Between *Irrational* and *Nonrational* Decisions

An *irrational* decision is one that is based on an absence of logical reasoning capabilities, whereas a *nonrational* decision is one that is made under uncertainty.[10] In other words, *nonrationality* is often used to describe bounded logical processes where a person has to make a choice without fully understanding the alternatives, probabilities, or consequences. This cognitive function cannot be controlled with premeditated thoughts, but it does draw from inherent logic based on acquired experience and cultivated intuition, which can be driven by emotions, or gut feelings. Basically, *nonrationality* describes the *mechanisms* behind limited rationality rather than the *outcomes* of the person's decision-making strategies.

The Polyvagal Perspective

A polyvagal perspective is a conceptualized framework for describing the evolutionary transition of social and homeostatic mechanisms in different physiological states.[11] Stephen Porges explains that the best way to understand the theory is to view it as a Rubik's cube puzzle with surfaces that represent different disciplines. In addition, these disciplines can be altered depending on newly added information. To solve the puzzle, one needs to understand how the autonomic nervous system evolved to perform defensive actions and support social interactions during different states. With the advancement of the theory and the inquiry into new questions, it came to replace predominant theories associated with cognitive behavior.

Traditionally, the Polyvagal Theory was developed as an attempt to shift the objectives of scientific research from a descriptive scientific orientation to a focus on the psychological and physiological processes. As a result, the Polyvagal Theory integrates the findings of researchers such as twentieth-century neurologist John Hughlings Jackson, who hypothesized that autonomic nervous responses function in a manner where older circuits inhibit the newer ones.[12] As a result, the newest evolutionary systems that support social engagement in a safe environment can be dampened to give precedence to the systems that support mobilization and immobilization. During times of extreme danger and fear, the human body automatically switches to the most primitive state of freeze to ensure survival.

The Polyvagal Theory underscores the links between the human autonomic nervous system (ANS) and cognitive mechanisms. According to Porges, the Polyvagal Theory relies on *neuroception* to inhibit or trigger the human body's defensive responses.[13]

Neuroception describes the process through which the human body determines whether the person requires a specific physiological response based on the surrounding environment. These states are usually labeled the sympathetic and parasympathetic states. The sympathetic state describes the condition where the human body has perceived an external threat that demands a flight-or-fight response, whereas the parasympathetic state describes the state of normalcy where the human body facilitates normal physical functions.[14] In such cases, neuroception allows the human body to determine the optimal response to handling sympathetic or parasympathetic nerve functions.

Evolutionary-focused neuroanatomists claim that the ANS originally consisted of a single dorsal vagal system, but this system has evolved to include the SNS and VVC, respectively, which became vital components of the ANS (see Figure 1.1 earlier in chapter). Researchers believe this is the fundamental hypothesis used to explain the evolution of mammals in the last 500 million years.[15] Figure 1.2 illustrates how the ANS system was conceptualized by integrating new functions layered over older ones in the mammalian organism.

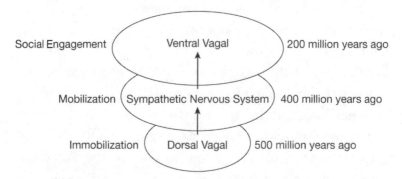

Figure 1.2 The Evolution of the Mammalian Autonomic Nervous System

Source: Dana, D. (2020, p. 32). *Polyvagal Exercises for Safety and Connection: 50 Client-Centered Practices (Norton Series on Interpersonal Neurobiology).* WW Norton & Company.

In her book *Polyvagal Exercises for Safety and Connection*, Deb Dana highlights the most comprehensive framework for the Polyvagal Theory. She explains that the autonomic nervous system is composed of two key branches: the parasympathetic and the sympathetic nerves.[16] However, the parasympathetic nerves are further subclassified into two pathways consisting of the dorsal vagal complex (DVC) and the ventral vagal complex (VVC). Accordingly, the ANS seems to be dependent on two branches and three pathways that control survival (see Figure 1.3).

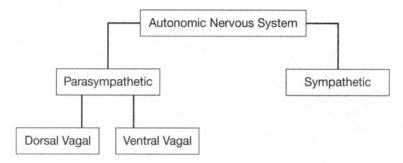

Figure 1.3 The Basic Structure of the Autonomic Nervous System

Source: Dana, D. (2020, p. 32). *Polyvagal Exercises for Safety and Connection: 50 Client-Centered Practices (Norton Series on Interpersonal Neurobiology).* WW Norton & Company.

Figure 1.3 can be broken down further to explain the roles and functions of the sympathetic and parasympathetic pathways (see Figure 1.4). In the graphic, the parasympathetic pathways are shown to support either social engagement or immobilization, whereas the sympathetic pathway supports mobilization in accordance with the flight-or-fight response.

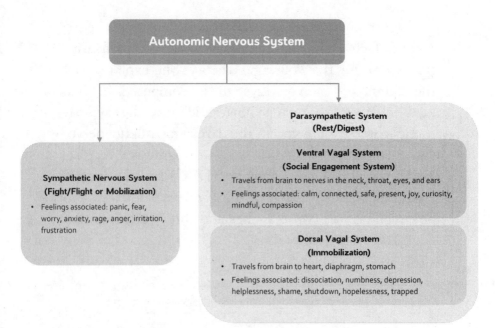

Figure 1.4 Comparison Between the Sympathetic and Parasympathetic Nervous Systems

Source: Issue 48 Quick Bytes: Trauma Network for Children Part 1: Polyvagal Theory, https://www.healthxchange.sg/childtraumanetwork/Documents/Quick%20Bytes/ Quick%20Bytes%20Issue%2048%20-%20Polyvagal%20Theory%20Part%201.pdf

While this information might remind you, either fondly or not so much, of high school science, the theory is quite revolutionary in terms of giving us a framework to make these systems work for us. Rather than being an unwilling passenger on Coney Island's Cyclone, being unknowingly conveyed by their autonomic nervous system, leaders can be the ride operator who ensures everyone's safe landing. All this takes is an awareness that our bodies and minds are built to adapt to our environment, and with awareness of our basic functions, we can create desired outcomes through integrated decision-making.

The Hierarchy of Autonomic Nervous Functions

The Polyvagal Theory highlights the hierarchy of nervous system functions with a focus on socialization (safe and relaxed), mobilization (fight or flight), or immobilization (shutdown). Beauchaine et al. (2007) performed a study on the phylogenetic hierarchy of ANS functions among children and adolescents.[17] (*Phylogenetic* relates to the evolutionary development and diversification of a group of organisms.) The researchers claimed that the human body responds to threats by going through a sequence of most advanced to most primitive response, especially when the chosen response does not achieve the desired impact.[18] For example, if social engagement is not sufficient for coping with a threat or extreme stimulus, the human body will move to the next response in the phylogenetic hierarchy: mobilization. Likewise, if the fight-or-flight response is ineffective, the human body will initiate the immobilization state and mediate the outcome based on the preceding response state. These three states explain that the ANS responds to threats by following the three states identified in the Polyvagal Theory, as follows:

1. Socialization and Safety
When a person feels safe and relaxed, the human body relies on the VVC (through the ventral nucleus of the vagus nerve) and the social engagement system to control socialization and feelings of safety in response to the surrounding environment. Anatomically, this pathway is controlled and regulated by the VVC by controlling the striated muscles of the head and face through the

trigeminal, vagus, and facial nerves.[19] These components are interconnected to support the social engagement system through facial expression, eye contact, breathing, vocalization, and listening. In addition to the nerves involved in the VVC, we can also see body language that expresses a sense of safety and connection, with a more relaxed and open presentation visible.

2. Mobilization

When a person believes there is danger or an impending threat, the human body triggers the flight-or-fight response in order to survive until the person can return to a safe environment. This action is primarily dependent on the SNS, which innervates the thoracic and upper lumbar spinal segments (which consist of the salivary and digestive organs).[20] The activation of the SNS can lead to a state of increased attention or activity aligned with the flight-or-fight response. In this state, heart rate and blood pressure increase while the lower body begins glycogenesis and ceases gastrointestinal peristalsis.[21] More simply, the human body dedicates more resources to metabolic functions that support fight or flight rather than normal baseline functions.

3. Immobilization

When the human body concludes that it is impossible or unrealistic to escape from a threat, it activates the DVC through the dorsal nucleus of the vagus nerve, thereby leading to a state of dissociation or collapse of the human body. This function is one of the oldest and most primitive functions of the ANS. The DVC primarily innervates the organs lying below the diaphragm.[22] As explained by the Polyvagal Theory, the DVC disrupts digestive functions to conserve metabolic resources and allocate them to organs that support the fight-or-flight response. In addition, the DVC can cause major disruptions to organ functions to the extent of inducing involuntary urination or defecation when the body is immobilized. While the last instance isn't likely to happen in the professional setting (barring a natural catastrophe or life-threatening encounter), immobilization is a state leaders and workers may find themselves in when they are too caught up in trying to make decisions that guarantee a desired future outcome.

The Polyvagal Ladder

While much of the existing literature on the Polyvagal Theory might cause a layperson's eyes to gloss over, Dana's work makes it much more accessible to a general audience. In her book *The Polyvagal Theory in Therapy*, she illustrates the transition across the physiological states with the Polyvagal Ladder (see Figure 1.5). This ladder narrows down the influences of the Polyvagal Theory on everyday experiences by categorizing the states according to three classifications: top, middle, and bottom. Keep in mind, however, that this is not a three-rung ladder, as there are varying levels of intensity of each state. In any event, these categories correspond to the three stages of the polyvagal hierarchy. To examine these concepts through various lenses, we will consider each position on the ladder from the perspective of our friend Oliver Green followed by general commentary.

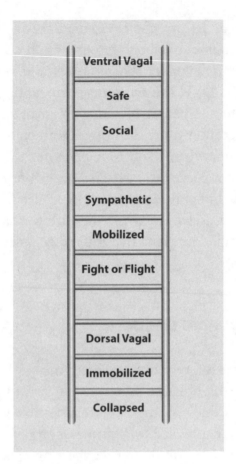

Figure 1.5 The Polyvagal Ladder

Source: Dana, D. (2018, p. 20). *The Polyvagal Theory in Therapy: Engaging the Rhythm of Regulation (Norton Series on Interpersonal Neurobiology).* WW Norton & Company.

1. The Top of the Ladder (Ventral Vagal): "What Does It Feel like to Be Safe and Social?"

Oliver Green's promotion to senior executive was unexpected and shocking, considering there had never been a senior executive as young as he was in the history of the company. However, Oliver felt he was up to the task. His promotion came with various benefits and privileges, such as managing a new workforce and handling additional responsibilities. In the first couple of months, his enthusiasm for the role made him a warm and engaging boss who could comfortably interact with both high-level and low-level workers.

When people stand at the top of the ladder, they feel safe, so they are likely to rely on the social engagement system through the parasympathetic nerve and the ventral vagal pathway.[23] As a result, the feelings people derive from their sense of safety and social connections allow them to concentrate on the bigger picture. The main activities involved during this state are balanced between rational decision-making such as being organized, being productive at work, and managing overall health and well-being and nonrational processes such as creativity, curiosity, exploration, and open connection with others. This state offers significant benefits in terms of improving heart rate, blood pressure, sleeping patterns, and digestion and strengthening the immune system.[24] These feelings and benefits change when a person experiences a threat that compels them to step down the ladder. However, in this state at the top of the ladder, a person has the ability to draw from both rational and nonrational thought processes because their bodies follow the normal neural pathways. In addition, the homeostatic and physiological functions remain steady, thereby allowing the person to make optimal decisions in their professional environment.

2. Moving Down the Ladder (Sympathetic): "I Feel Fear. Should I Fight or Run?"

Over the next six months, Oliver gradually lost his enthusiasm for the position. His supervisors' expectations seemed unrealistic, and dealing with employees was more challenging than he had initially expected. Despite attempts to resolve his predicament, he usually felt stressed and anxious and found himself losing his temper more often and taking more personal days off. He disliked the work environment and the conflicts that emerged on a daily basis. He was having trouble getting a good night's sleep and difficulty concentrating during the day. Though he loved the perks and the salary, he regretted his promotion to senior executive due to the increased workload and stress levels.

When a person experiences a threat that induces fear or other extreme negative emotions, the sympathetic branch of the ANS activates and encourages the person to take action. The most common responses in this stage include increased heart rate, short and shallow breaths, and regular scans of the surrounding environment to identify danger.[25] The flow of adrenaline in the bloodstream is one of the leading causes of these responses. In addition, the person may experience anxiety, anger, panic attacks, or disorientation due to the situation. These activities are classified under mobilization. The main long-term consequences of this step down the ladder are risk for heart disease, elevated blood pressure, sleeping problems, high cholesterol, memory impairment, stomach problems, muscle tension, and increased vulnerability to illnesses. Overall, it can be perceived that the mobilization stage of the Polyvagal Ladder is associated with adverse health implications.

At this stage of the ladder, the world may feel chaotic, unfriendly, or dangerous. As a result, people who experience mobilization may make spontaneous decisions that are usually oriented toward removing or evading the threat. These decisions may or may not be the best choice in a particular situation.

3. At the Bottom of the Ladder (Dorsal Vagal): "If I Can't Fight or Run, What Should I Do?"

With fewer than three months left till the one-year anniversary of his promotion, Oliver found himself freezing up anytime an important decision needed to be made. He had tried various strategies to reduce his stress levels and deal with his increased workload without success. During conflicts, he also found himself shutting down. His supervisors were concerned whether Oliver's promotion had been premature. His subordinates also noticed that Oliver didn't seem up to the challenge of leading the department. In fact, the entire organization believes that "freezing" is a sign of a weak leader—and that's exactly how Oliver saw himself now.

People who reach the bottom of the ladder often experience danger or threats that are too overwhelming to face. As a result, the human body returns to the most primitive state of the ANS. In this state, the parasympathetic nerve is activated through the dorsal vagal pathway. This pathway is usually labeled the "primitive vagus" because it describes an autonomic nervous response that occurs when a person feels trapped or is unable to take action in the face of danger. The main outcome of this state is collapse, shutdown, or dissociation.[26] The body moves into a state of conservation where it drastically reduces metabolic activities in nonessential organs. The main behavioral responses in this state include hopelessness, feelings of abandonment, and disorientation. Furthermore, this state can cause longterm health consequences, including chronic fatigue, low blood pressure, weight gain, stomach problems, memory loss, and type 2 diabetes.

People at the bottom of the Polyvagal Ladder often experience debilitating levels of despair that prevent them from accessing logical thought processes. Their physical and cognitive limitations prevent them from identifying the best decision and may even keep them from recognizing what there is to choose from. Clearly, this situation can result in worse performance in the workplace compared to the first two stages of the Polyvagal Ladder.

Dysregulation in Neuroception

The scenarios just described illustrate different organizational situations that drive employees to experience the different states of the Polyvagal Ladder. For Oliver, the calm state results in optimal decision-making because the nervous system supports a balance between rational and nonrational decision-making. However, when Oliver becomes overwhelmed by his unfamiliar responsibilities and challenges, his stress begins to mount, causing his neuroception to become dysregulated in a self-reinforcing pattern. In other words, Oliver's dysregulation of neuroception—perceiving danger where none exists—encourages him to continue to identify threats. This only serves to keep him in a perpetual mobilization state and eventually pushes him toward the immobilization state. Oliver is no longer able to think clearly because, above all else, his brain simply wants him to survive the "danger."

Neuroception is an important function in the human body that allows individuals to determine whether situations pose a danger to them. Accordingly, as described by Oliver's scenario, dysregulation in neuroception can compel the body to go into a defensive state.[27] The most common indicators of dysregulation in another person include averting eye contact, fidgeting, abnormal movement and speech patterns, and social disengagement. As a result, this response creates a cascading effect that negatively impacts brain processes and overall decision-making. You can see that, in the professional environment, this would be detrimental to organizational productivity, staff satisfaction, and retention.

Human neurophysiology is designed to operate optimally when it perceives that the environment is safe. However, under stress or trauma, the body will release signals through neural systems to respond to the perceived threat.[28] The nervous system also transitions into the sympathetic state to respond to the perceived threat.

For that reason, decision-making can become skewed due to the body's perceptions of danger, particularly when it is difficult to ascertain whether or not real danger exists. This rationale explains why people who are nervous and tense in the workplace often experience challenges concentrating, listening, and retaining information. In the workplace, the sympathetic state encourages the worker to perceive survival as the top priority, thereby causing abnormal situations that can affect the work environment and overall staff productivity.

Considering that decision-making involves not only cognition, but also intuition and emotion, it can be perceived that regulation tends to affect both rational and nonrational decision-making. For some, decision-making becomes a dual process where the cognitive aspects merge with the emotional and intuitive aspects. As you should now understand, this is what an instinctive leader does. Soosalu et al. claim that the combination of emotional and intuitive aspects into one "experiential" entity is an important requirement for optimal decision-making.[29] We support that claim, as it can allow a leader to make reflexive decisions in accordance with their head, gut (instinct), and/or heart (emotions).

In Oliver Green's case, the more experienced colleagues were familiar with their organizational roles to the extent of being able to make reflexive decisions at a moment's notice. In comparison, Oliver was unable to merge his analytical and intuitive aspects because his lack of experience and trust in his instincts caused his ANS to react as if any challenge was a life-threatening incident. Because he hadn't yet learned how neuroception becomes dysregulated, he was unable to regulate in order to respond constructively. In addition to being uncomfortable relying on his gut instincts, the feeling of being in "over his head" caused Oliver's decision-making to deteriorate. His nervous system was in the sympathetic state, and each new challenge easily triggered him to be avoidant (flight) or confrontative (fight), and, in extreme cases, Oliver simply froze. Clearly, the cultivation of instinctive leadership, which relies on an understanding of the ANS's response to stress, is an effective solution for improving analytical and intuitive decision-making while also mitigating the negative effects of dysregulation in neuroception.

The Polyvagal Theory at a Glance

Components and dimensions: The vagal system represents three systems: ventral vagal complex (VVC), sympathetic nervous system (SNS), and dorsal vagal complex (DVC).

Nonrational thinking capabilities: The human vagal system supports physiological and heuristic values. In other words, it enables humans to learn and retain cognitive memory to support more successful decisions.

Nervous mechanisms: Physiological states mediated by the vagal system are determined by detection of safety within the immediate surroundings.

Neural/cognitive processes: Cognitive processes rely on neuroception to evaluate the risks of the immediate surroundings and to weight the vagal output to the connected areas of the nervous system.

Hierarchy: Depending on the environment, in response to any external or perceived stress the human body transitions through three states in this order: (1) socialization, (2) mobilization, and (3) immobilization.

Stress, Depression, Trauma, and Anxiety in the Workplace

Oliver Green's subordinates saw that, in his present condition, he was not up to task to lead them, solve disputes, or make good business decisions, which resulted in their own dissatisfaction with the work environment. In fact, one of his team members requested a transfer to another team, while another handed in a resignation letter.

Employees resign prematurely for numerous reasons. Some leave for personal reasons, while others resign due to organizational factors. In both cases, organizational leadership is a major cause of the employee turnover. An article published in the *Harvard Business Review* highlighted the problem this way: "People don't quit a job, the saying goes—they quit a boss."[30] This quote encapsulates the idea that poor leadership is one of the principal causes of low employee retention and high turnovers in the twenty-first century.

In the modern workplace, the employees' performance is usually dependent on their psychological well-being. While most organizations would prefer their employees to be in top shape, the reality is that employees' productivity can be negatively affected by their professional or personal problems. Issues such as stress, depression, trauma, and anxiety are common psychological issues that often pose negative influences on employees' well-being. A study also published by the *Harvard Business Review* in 2022 revealed that approximately 44 percent of employees experience stress in their work environments. These findings are relatively higher compared to previous years. The problems peaked in 2020 due to the accumulation of compounding factors, including worsening work conditions and the emergence of the Covid-19 pandemic. In the *State of the Global Workplace Report* published by Gallup in 2022, research shows that the prevalence of employee stress escalated in 2021. While sadness and anger declined marginally between the two years, many negative emotions remained at an all-time high.

The CEO of Gallup outlined that most people in the world spend an average of 81,396 hours working. Given this time frame, most people would expect that working has become an exciting undertaking. However, the report highlighted that 60 percent of workers around the world are emotionally detached, whereas 19 percent are miserable. The notion that "work sucks" is everywhere, and it has been the topic of ancient philosophers, world leaders, and regular members of the modern working community.[31] Other studies explain that mental health disorders are the leading causes of the global health burden. The GBD 2020 is a global ranking that estimates the burden of 370 different diseases and injuries and 88 risk factors across approximately 204 nations worldwide. The ranking also quantifies the adjusted life years to evaluate the number of years of healthy life that employees have lost due to illness. With that said, depression and anxiety were ranked among the 25 leading causes of health-related burden in 2019.[32] Stress and trauma have also illustrated similar patterns, thereby emphasizing the need to introduce strategies to improve employees' mental and emotional well-being in the workplace.

"Whether an illness affects your heart, your leg, or your brain, it's still an illness, and there should be no distinction,"said former first lady Michelle Obama on World Mental Health Day 2020.[33] The statement summarizes the challenges most employees expect to face on a daily basis. Most employees avoid discussing their mental health issues due to stigma or fear. In addition, these psychological issues can be amplified by intrinsic or extrinsic factors derived from the employee's personal or professional environment. Although society has adopted innovative means to address different mental health issues, stigma still surrounds those with a lived experience of mental illness. These psychological influences can pose severe challenges to organizational performance by negatively influencing employees' decision-making and overall productivity.

KEY POINTS

- The ventral vagal complex (VVC), sympathetic nervous system (SNS), and dorsal vagal complex (DVC) each play a vital role in controlling the body's responses to danger and other extreme emotional influences.
- Neuroception is the main trigger for determining whether the (1) VVC will support social engagement, (2) SNS will support mobilization for flight or fight, or (3) DVC will cause the body's immobilization. These responses are dependent on the surrounding cues of safety and danger.
- Dysregulation in neuroception is the perception of danger where none exists, priming the body for mobilization and possibly immobilization, which negatively affect one's decision-making ability.
- Situations of extreme stress, anger, fear, or anxiety can trigger changes in the person's autonomic state from social engagement to mobilization to immobilization. Instinctive leadership largely depends on a leader's ability to recognize the three autonomic states in the workplace and successfully navigate back to a state of socialization.

CHAPTER 2

Applying the Polyvagal Theory to Leadership

The rapid evolution of human resource management practices has encouraged researchers to investigate the main characteristics of successful leaders. While some leaders are born with innate leadership characteristics, a vast majority are slowly nurtured to portray the prerequisite competencies of a good leader. To explain how instinctive leadership can be cultivated, we focus on four popular leadership styles: transactional, transformational, servant, and situational leadership. We'll use our fictious senior executive Oliver Green to illustrate these leadership styles, imbuing him with various qualities that sometimes may conflict with what you've read previously and from scenario to scenario to suit the needs of the discussion. (Fortunately, Oliver is a good sport.) Given that leaders are often exposed to many challenges in their respective professions, we'll look at how stress, trauma, and constructs of the Polyvagal Theory can influence the decision-making of such leaders. This approach offers important insights into the best strategies for cultivating good leadership in a variety of modern professional scenarios. In brief, we aim to clarify how emotional and mental stimuli influence modern leadership outcomes.

Leadership in the Twenty-First Century

The principal factor that contributed to Oliver Green's promotion to senior executive was his good leadership skills. Oliver has taken several leadership courses, so he understands the strengths and weaknesses of different leadership strategies. As a result, his good performance was quickly recognized by his superiors, who acknowledged the importance of embracing new and innovative leadership approaches. While Oliver often relies on his theoretical knowledge to make decisions, he understands the importance of instinctive leadership. From his perspective, an effective leader should be capable of weighing the benefits and risks of decisions in a manner that positively supports his subordinates' growth.

In the leadership field, several questions have confounded researchers and scholars since the nineteenth century:

Who is a leader?
Are good leaders born or made?
What characteristics define a good leader?

The evolution of modern leadership concepts made it more challenging to answer these questions. Research by Hunt and Fedynich offers important insights into the different responses offered to those questions.[1] On one hand, some researchers argue that good leaders are born with the innate ability to lead; on the other hand, skeptics claim that leaders are cultivated by instilling knowledge and experience. However, a few extremists believe there is no such thing as a leader because leadership is a fictional construct.[2] Despite these perspectives, the reality is that leadership is still a mysterious construct because there is no one-size-fits-all strategy that can allow leaders to achieve good outcomes in every organizational setting.

Fundamentally, most leaders make decisions by focusing on the intrinsic and extrinsic factors surrounding the organizational environment. This ideology is the traditional view of leadership, which encourages the belief that leadership depends on a person's ability to make rational decisions in their respective professional scenario. For instance, it is well known that most leaders struggle with dilemmas that can be resolved using analytical decision-making, such as simultaneously balancing financial performance and organizational productivity. However, few leaders understand the mental and emotional toll that emerges due to these choices. In some cases, the choices can cause dysregulation in neuroception and cause a person to alternately shift between the sympathetic and parasympathetic states without awareness. Emotional regulation and dysregulation are important influences of cognitive decision-making.[3] Hence, modern leaders need to embrace leadership strategies that provide a holistic view of their applications and outcomes.

The inadequacy of research regarding intuitive decision-making is a critical problem in the modern professional environment. Researchers define *intuition* as a decision-making mechanism that relies on the rapid and nonconscious recognition of associations and patterns to make effective judgments.[4] Intuitive and rational decision-making are prerequisites of good decision-making, but traditional research often highlights the tension between the two constructs instead of their conjoint use. With that said, the field of neuroscience has become a vital discipline for explaining the neural and nervous system responses aligned with leadership and professional decision-making.[5] By focusing on common emotional influences, it is possible to explain how most workers make decisions when in either the sympathetic state or the parasympathetic state.

Rational and Nonrational Decision-Making in Leadership

Oliver Green has become quite popular in his company since he was promoted to senior executive. He acknowledges that the leadership position is quite challenging because he is often forced to make decisions he disagrees with. For instance, firing workers is considered the most difficult task in the department. Such decisions require Oliver to approach the decision from both rational and nonrational perspectives. The rational perspective highlights that the organization needs to lay off some workers to optimize the use of resources, and the two underperforming employees are the obvious choices to let go. Despite this, Oliver personally likes these two employees and feels conflicted about the decision. However, if the remainder of employees are performing at the same basic level, the nonrational perspective gives him insight into whom to lay off while also giving him the ability to be sympathetic to the workers and their needs. Oliver's knowledge of the workers' challenges outside the office is limited—perhaps laying someone off may aggravate their personal challenges at home or, alternatively, perhaps that worker has a fallback plan in the case of a layoff. Without knowing all the particulars, Oliver must trust his gut that he's making the right decision. Thus, in this scenario, he needs to balance rational and nonrational considerations. He needs to ensure that his personal feelings do not interfere with making the most appropriate business decision.

As you learned in Chapter 1, the Polyvagal Theory highlights the correlation between the autonomic nervous system and decision-making. Accordingly, decision-making in the modern professional environment often occurs through rational or nonrational mechanisms. Rational decision-making is often classified as the orthodox mechanism of decision-making in the professional environment.[6] This approach is underpinned by analytical and conscious reasoning capabilities. In comparison, nonrational decision-making is often classified as the unorthodox view. This perspective argues that intuition (as well as spirituality) is a legitimate means through which leaders make organizational choices.

Fortunately, another branch of decision-making has surfaced that merges rational and nonrational decision-making, which, as you have likely concluded, is the essential element of instinctive leadership. Integrated decision-making combines the strengths of rational and nonrational decision-making, thereby improving decision-making outcomes.[7] In other words, integrated decision-making encourages leaders to combine analytical and intuitive decision-making strategies, as illustrated in Figure 2.1.

The four leadership approaches we'll be exploring in this chapter differ in terms of their reliance on rational and nonrational decision-making. Foremost, transactional leaders tend to rely on rational decision-making. Contrarily, transformational leaders and situational leaders utilize the integrated approach, which merges rational and nonrational choices. With regard to servant leaders, these professionals are characterized by their reliance on nonrational decision-making, especially spirituality. These leadership styles have different intrinsic and extrinsic influences that affect their outcomes.

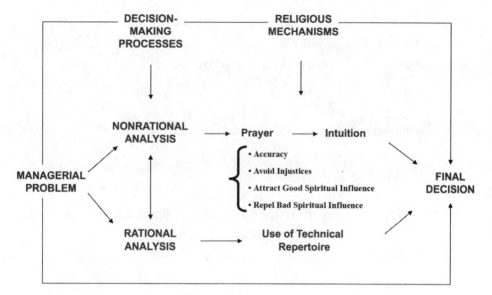

Figure 2.1 Integration of Rational and Nonrational Decision-Making in Leaders

Source: Vasconcelos, A.F. (2009). Intuition, prayer, and managerial decision-making processes: A religion-based framework, *Management Decision 47*(6), 930–949.

Popular Leadership Styles

In the modern professional environment, there are numerous leadership styles and classifications: transactional, transformational, servant, situational, authoritarian, delegative, democratic, charismatic, and laissez-faire leadership. In addition, some leadership strategies have emerged that share the characteristics of two or more leadership strategies. To stay on task, we'll focus on just the four mentioned in the previous section: transactional, transformational, servant, and situational leadership. We've chosen these styles because they reflect the main characteristics of decision-making in the socialization state of the Polyvagal Ladder (see Chapter 1). We'll place

Oliver Green in hypothetical scenarios for each style to illustrate the strengths and weaknesses of each. After we've discussed each style at length, we will revisit them through the lens of the Polyvagal Theory.

Transactional Leadership

"Oliver the Machine"

Because Oliver is the youngest senior executive, his performance is usually under strict supervision by his superiors and work rivals. To ensure that he maintains optimal productivity at the workplace, Oliver creates a work environment that emphasizes efficiency. In his department, everyone follows the organization's rules "to the letter." When comparing performance, he does not look for average performance; he always wants the best. As a result, his department has consistently delivered good performance due to his strict leadership. In return, Oliver is very generous with employee benefits. Good employees are highly rewarded, whereas low-performing employees often receive corresponding punishments. Oliver prefers this leadership style because he values strict compliance to organizational rules but feels that any deviation will negatively affect productivity. Most employees feel that Oliver is a cold and calculating machine.

However, a few months later, Oliver starts to notice a decline in organizational performance. His subordinates often arrive late, while others have become demotivated. Oliver begins to offer greater rewards for employees who improve their performance and greater punishments for those who fail. However, this change further worsens job dissatisfaction in his department. The company's budget prevents him from increasing employee benefits, so he has been unable to figure out the best solution for his predicament. Should he abandon transactional leadership, or should he alter future rewards and punishments?

The transactional leadership style is the oldest and most popular leadership style. This style argues that leadership primarily depends on exchange processes to elicit desired behaviors in subordinate workers. In *Building a Culture of Conscious Leadership*, authors David Potter and Jens Starke claim that transactional leadership occurs when the leader exchanges something that has political, economic, and psychological value with a follower.[8] Most transactional leaders utilize strict managerial approaches to supervise their employees instead of visionary strategies oriented toward improving employee behaviors.[9] These leaders often develop rigid work environments characterized by articulated roles and responsibilities. In addition, the leader often expects the employee to adhere to the organization's rules and regulations. For that reason, the transactional leadership approach is usually associated with contingent-based management systems.

The transactional leadership style can be enacted through passive or active management. Aga outlines that "active management by exception" describes the form of management where the transactional leader promotes purely functional work interactions.[10] As a result, the leader offers corrective action when the problem has escalated to the extent of being brought to the leader or if it can no longer be ignored. These leaders prefer the laissez-faire leadership approach. In comparison, "active management by exception" involves the transactional leader actively supervising the employees' work and providing immediate corrective action.[11] The leader actively seeks flaws or weaknesses in the employees' performance. These two leadership approaches share a common attribute—there is low personal identification between the leader and the subordinate.

An important feature of transactional leadership involves the use of rewards and punishments to improve employee motivation. This leadership style is based on the assumption that employees value extrinsic motivation. Benefits such as money, recognition, status, promotions, support, and company perks are the most common sources of extrinsic motivation in the modern organizational environment.[12] These benefits are usually established in accordance with the organization's guidelines and protocols. In addition, these benefits can be classified according to pecuniary and nonpecuniary benefits,[13] or constructive or nonconstructive corrections.[14] Overall, transactional leadership is based on the idea that extrinsic motivation can improve organizational productivity by appealing to the workers' self-interest.

Strengths and Weaknesses of Transactional Leadership

Although the transactional leadership approach is supported by significant research, the style has several weaknesses, but let's consider the strengths first. The most important strength is that it relies on credible organizational strategies to inspire subordinates and induce commitment.[15] The benefits are amplified when it is merged with transformational leadership because the style supports favorable individual and organizational outcomes. Another benefit is that the contingent-based reward systems often appeal to the followers' self-interest. As a result, the organization can use various methods that are "tried and tested" by modern researchers. Furthermore, research also shows that the transactional leadership style offers significant results in environments where deviant behavior negatively affects organizational outcomes.[16] For instance, breaking protocol in the healthcare setting can cause the loss of a patient. Overall, the transactional leadership style has been embraced by many leaders because it augments the leader's authority, stimulates productivity, and encourages conformity to organizational rules.

Transactional leadership is often criticized because of its outcomes. Although most leaders expect strong rewards by using this leadership approach, they often generate expected levels of performance instead of outstanding performance.[17] In other words, the use of transactional leadership can indirectly limit organizational productivity. Another weakness is that transactional leadership often neglects the employees' intrinsic needs.[18] For instance, self-actualization and esteem are not prioritized in this leadership style, which can result in job dissatisfaction.[19] Other researchers have claimed that transactional leadership leads to unequal distribution of power between leaders and subordinates.[20] These findings explain that transactional leadership supports rational and contingent-based decision-making, but this approach is also its greatest weakness.

Transformational Leadership

"Oliver the Idol"

Oliver's superiors have high expectations for his performance, and they feel he will quickly rise through the ranks. Oliver also feels the same, so he is willing to dedicate his time and effort to building the perfect work environment for his workers. To achieve this goal, Oliver holds regular weekly meetings in his department to check on the employees' well-being and their current progress. He also uses the meetings to discuss his experiences and his professional journey before becoming the youngest senior executive in the company. When assigning work responsibilities, he places emphasis on the employees' strengths and weaknesses, and he always offers feedback to his subordinates. Most workers aspire to be like Oliver, so they often work long hours to meet targets. Accordingly, the department has noticed that performance has been gradually improving. Overall, Oliver has created the image that he is an idol: the best role model in the company.

Despite recording good performance for several months, however, Oliver's department starts to record unusual fluctuations in overall performance. During some months, his department records the best performance, but in others, his department is the worst. This problem emerges because some workers are strongly motivated to deliver the best work, while others seem demotivated. In addition, many employees have become reluctant to comply with organizational rules, arriving late at work and refusing to follow company protocols. Oliver feels that his leadership is too relaxed.

Should Oliver abandon the transformational leadership style, or should he pursue other methods of employee motivation?

After transactional leadership, transformational leadership is considered the second most popular leadership style in modern society. Reliable research highlights that transformational leaders drive their followers to think beyond immediate self-interest through inspiration, idealized influence, charisma, or intellectual stimulation.[21] Accordingly, the transformational leadership style is the polar opposite of transactional leadership because it requires the leader to use intrinsic motivation to inspire followers instead of extrinsic constructs. Transformational leadership requires strong and visionary leaders who have the ability to rally subordinates to support a well-articulated vision.[22] For that reason, it is common for transformational leaders to dedicate significant amounts of time to inspiring their subordinates to support the organization's core values.[23] This leadership style is more inclusive than the transactional approach.

Transformational leadership can be achieved by aligning organizational activities to the company's vision or modeling the work behaviors toward specific core values. Research shows that transformational leaders usually focus on increased recognition of the employees' competencies, strengths, and weaknesses.[24] As a result, it is possible to create meaningful relationships between leaders and subordinates. If a leader can be accepted as a role model in the workplace, it will be possible to have idealized influence over the workforce. The leader can achieve the same goal by nurturing trust and communication with the employees.[25] Research also shows that transformational leaders promote creativity and innovation when solving long-standing issues or developing strategies for optimizing organizational performance during times of uncertainty.[26] Although these findings do not indicate whether transformational leadership is superior to transactional leadership, it highlights that the former is particularly suited to improve employee motivation.

Strengths and Weaknesses of Transformational Leadership
Like transactional leadership, the transformational leadership approach is oriented toward improving organizational productivity. While transactional leadership focuses on optimizing corporate performance, the transformational style centers on the employees' well-being. Some researchers have discerned that there are direct correlations between transformational leadership and organizational performance.[27] In comparison, other scholars have claimed that transformational leadership inspires creativity and innovation in the workplace, thereby augmenting organizational productivity.[28] Moreover, transformational leadership encourages senior employees to not only monitor their subordinates' behavior but also create opportunities for exchanging knowledge and nurturing useful skills.[29] Evidently, these strengths are primarily oriented toward improving employee satisfaction and retention.

Despite the presumed benefits of transformational leadership, it has been criticized for several weaknesses.

Foremost, transformational leadership is known to foster individual idealized influence, while relegating group-level processes.[30] In other words, the leader is often encouraged to focus on individual employees and neglect external considerations such as resource management and stakeholder engagement. In addition, research published by Banks et al. underscores the ambiguity behind the definition and characteristics of transformational leadership.[31] The scholars reveal that transformational leadership is relatively broad; thus, there is a lot of uncertainty surrounding the drivers of employee behavior in real-life scenarios. These weaknesses demonstrate that transformational leadership is an ideal strategy for managing workers, but little is known about its universal applications and the different situational variables that should be considered.

Servant Leadership

"Oliver the Servant"

Oliver has developed a reputation for being good not only at stock trading but also at handling employee interactions. He believes that the best way to improve productivity in his department is to create a conducive work environment for workers. Oliver always listens to his employees' problems, and he prides himself on helping his followers when they experience problems at work or at home. Accordingly, Oliver has created an open environment for his workers. His employees are encouraged to discuss and exchange ideas among themselves. Although he encourages competition between workers, he always encourages his subordinates to be morally upright. Due to these actions, Oliver has noticed a marginal improvement in his staff's performance. In a nutshell, Oliver is envisioned as a servant leader in the company.

Although Oliver's department has noticed an increase in productivity, the growth rate is not aligned with expectations. The department has not achieved the milestones that the workers previously established. Furthermore, Oliver has noticed that workers often waste a lot of time discussing and exchanging ideas, which negatively affects their productivity. To solve these problems, Oliver is considering whether he should introduce stricter rules and restrictions for his employees.

Should Oliver abandon the servant leadership style, or should he dedicate more time to improving the staff's needs?

The servant leadership style is a newly emergent concept that encourages leaders to focus on the welfare of their employees instead of on their personal glory or organizational benefits. In this context, it is essential to clarify a long-standing myth surrounding servant leadership. Many people assume that servant leadership requires leaders to be subservient to their followers. However, this is a myth because servant leadership involves inspiring workers by appealing to their virtues and personal values.[32] Research shows that servant leaders often use their power and authority to strengthen their employees' autonomy.[33] Most servant leaders dedicate their time to interacting with, educating, and inspiring their subordinates.[34] The overall objective of servant leadership is to ensure that employees reach their best potential.

The creation of a positive organization is dependent on the altruistic motives of the senior management. Accordingly, servant leadership is usually associated with creating a culture of spirituality in which the "greater good" is factored in. The interactions between the servant leader and the employees are oriented toward promoting support and collaboration without self-interest.[35] These interactions create a positive environment that nurtures good organizational virtues through constructive human impact, moral goodness, and social betterment. On this note, servant leadership is grounded on the leader's use of trust and shared decision-making to mediate the staff's self-serving and opportunistic characteristics.[36] Overall, the main distinction between servant leadership and other styles lies in its emphasis on selflessly serving others instead of self-service.

Strengths and Weaknesses of Servant Leadership

Servant leadership is a controversial style of leadership that has become the topic of many research studies. Research shows that the servant leadership style has been embraced by many professionals due to its ability to strengthen organizational productivity. Specchia et al. outline that servant leadership can optimize productivity by merging different professional competencies: collective decision-making, teamwork, and ethics.[37] In addition, servant leadership involves simple leadership constructs and strategies. In comparison, the transactional and transformational approaches require the leader to use complex strategies to determine extrinsic and intrinsic rewards, respectively. The servant leader sacrifices rewards and personal advancement to improve staff productivity and organizational performance.

Concerning the weaknesses, servant leadership is surrounded by a lot of uncertainty. Although numerous studies have been published focusing on servant leadership, there is no universal strategy for determining the definition and characteristics of servant leadership. This problem is highlighted by Winston and Fields, who argue that there is little consensus in the descriptions and real-life applications of servant leadership.[38] Most definitions have discrepancies in their description of trust, humility, love, wisdom, healing, and spirituality.[39] The vague description and classifications of servant leadership hamper its successful implementation in real-life professional settings.

Situational Leadership

"Oliver the Problem-Solver"

As senior executive, Oliver is often assigned important human resource management responsibilities in addition to managing stock trade transactions. Correspondingly, he uses a leadership style that focuses on leader-follower engagement. He regularly interacts with all new and existing workers to understand their strengths, weaknesses, and individual needs. As a result, he often gains important insights that can improve his department's productivity. Furthermore, he always offers assistance and guidance to the workers depending on their respective needs.

Although it was difficult to improve productivity in the initial stages of his leadership position, Oliver's department started achieving major milestones. He understands his employees to the extent of delegating responsibilities using his gut instincts.

Although his leadership strategy has been quite successful, Oliver often fails to distinguish how to offer direction and support to his subordinates. For instance, new workers require more basic levels of support than experienced workers, but experienced workers often require support that is aligned with their specific issues. Oliver fears that it is impractical to interact with and understand *all* his employees.

Should Oliver abandon the situational leadership style, or should he continue to offer support and direction to all subordinates in his department?

The situational leadership style emerged in reaction to trait-based leadership approaches. Traditionally, researchers believed that situational leadership could be nurtured by dedicating adequate levels of time and resources to nurture the core leadership traits. Accordingly, the situational leadership style was conceptualized to create a coherent structure for the life cycle of leadership.[40] In this approach, leaders use directiveness to deal with new employees, and then they gradually substitute directiveness with support.[41] The definition of situational leadership emerged from these two roles: a leadership style that merges both directive and supportive dimensions in a given situation.[42] As employees become more competent in their respective positions, the need for support gradually declines.

Situational leaders place a lot of emphasis on guiding their employees using appropriate methods. For instance, the situational leader interacts with the employee by analyzing their performance and partnering with them to improve performance. Thus, the leader needs to be flexible in order to offer assistance that matches the employee's developmental level.[43] Although significant research has been performed on the different leadership strategies used by modern leaders, most of the concepts are impractical from the viewpoint of situational leadership.[44] Most theories emphasize improved performance, but few of them describe the appropriate levels of support leaders need to offer to subordinates. Accordingly, situational leadership addresses this gap by ensuring the leader offers support that conforms with the employees' capabilities.

Strengths and Weaknesses of Situational Leadership

Situational leadership has been adopted by many modern organizations, but many concerns are still raised about its weaknesses. With regard to the strengths, the situational leadership style is the most appropriate approach for training and academic-oriented activities.[45] It relies on a well-structured framework for instilling knowledge and skills in employees: support and direction. The leader can support these two roles depending on the surrounding environment. Inexperienced employees often require high directive behavior and low support, whereas more experienced workers demand low directive behavior and high support.[46] In conclusion, the situational leadership theory reveals that different employees require varying leadership styles that match their development levels.

The situational leadership style is inherently limited by the inadequacy of evidence-based research supporting its applications. Over the years, many revisions have been performed on situational leadership that have increased the complexity of the model.[47] The lack of empirical evidence to justify the concept's validity has increased the uncertainty of the concept's weakness. Overall, while it is well known that situational leadership supports employee training and coaching, few studies support its empirical utility and validity.

Comparing the Four Leadership Styles

The differences and similarities between the leadership styles is shown in Table 2.1, based on the following categories: leadership strategy, focus and orientation, followers' motivation, leader's actions, organizational goals, creativity and innovation, and neuroscience perspective. While the comparison between transactional and transformational leadership is relatively straightforward, delineating the characteristics of the servant and situational leadership styles becomes more challenging. Nevertheless, we've included the accepted basics to provide you with an overview that provides important insight moving forward.

Table 2.1 Comparison of Leadership Styles

	Transactional	Transformational	Servant	Situational
Leadership strategy	Leaders encourage followers by appealing to their self-interest and personal desires.	Leaders encourage followers by driving them to support the organization's best interests.	Leaders serve followers by resolving their problems and fulfilling their personal needs.	Leaders encourage followers to adapt to different situations.
Focus and orientation	Focuses on meeting current organizational objectives.	Focuses on pursuing long-term organizational objectives.	Focuses on followers' and organizational values.	Focuses on instilling knowledge in followers.
Followers' motivation	Followers are motivated by the organization's rewards and punishments.	Followers are motivated by idealistic goals and good organizational values.	Followers are motivated by the leader's vision of organizational growth.	Followers are motivated by the need to adapt to their respective work environments.
Leader's actions	Leader's responsive actions are usually strict and bureaucratic.	Leader's responsive actions are usually adaptive and practical.	Leader's responsive actions occurs through positive-reinforcement strategies.	Leader's actions are usually flexible based on the follower's needs.
Organizational goals	The organization pursues stability and consistent performance.	The organization aims to respond to turbulent situations and improve sharing of power between leader and followers.	The organization pursues the sharing of power between leader and followers.	The organization aims to respond to human resource issues.
Creativity and innovation	Leader does not emphasize creativity and innovation.	Leader emphasizes creativity and innovation.	Leader emphasizes creativity and innovation.	Leader emphasizes creativity and innovation under direct supervision.
Neuroscience perspective	Followers derive satisfaction from the fulfillment of their personal and professional needs.	Followers value the organization's vision, which drives them to improve productivity.	Followers value the mental and emotional rewards that are provided by the leader.	Followers derive value from gaining knowledge and adapting to the work environment.

VanderPal, G., and R. Brazie, Exploratory Study of Polyvagal Theory and Underlying Stress and Trauma That Influence Major Leadership Approaches, *Journal of Applied Business and Economics* 24, no. 1 (2022).

As you can see from this table, although there are some similarities in a category or two, each leadership style has a unique profile. When a leader adopts any one of these strategies for an adequate length of time, there isn't much deviation in their daily interactions with employees. For example, a leader who is strict and bureaucratic one day generally won't suddenly be adaptive and flexible the next. And, while some employees may not resonate with a certain leadership style, they at least know what to expect on an *ordinary* day.

The Effect of Mobilization and Immobilization on Decision-Making

In each of the previous scenarios and discussions of leadership styles, the characteristics of organizational decision-making are viewed from the parasympathetic state, the socialization rung on the Polyvagal Ladder. In this state, leaders make decisions in safe environments that allow them to make effective decisions. These decisions are also less susceptible to bias and discrimination. However, in the sympathetic state, the mobilization section of the ladder, decision-making mechanisms become skewed. In this state, integrated decision-making functions decline, increasing the chance of making poor choices. So, when stress and trauma compel the autonomic nervous system to shift from the parasympathetic state to the sympathetic state, leaders' decisions can be adversely affected if they lack awareness on how to return to a balanced state. Let's consider Oliver again.

After Oliver Green's promotion, he was assigned various new responsibilities. His supervisors informed him that they had high expectations of his future performance—and so did he. For that reason, Oliver dedicated a lot of time and effort to improving organizational productivity using his tried-and-true analytical problem-solving strategies. Having never been in a leadership role before, he struggled to find a way to relate to and supervise his employees. He'd read about various leadership strategies and had taken courses, but he couldn't find his stride to the point where his department was experiencing consistent rewards.

As the months wore on, Oliver's stress level increased. His subordinates complained to HR that he was too temperamental and sometimes impolite. What's more, having to make major decisions increased Oliver's anxiety tenfold, and then no one wanted to approach him with even the simplest work matter. The worst was when Oliver had to fire two employees in his depart-ment. He froze. He could not decide how to approach terminating the contracts of employees who had been working under him for a year—and how would he choose which employees to let go? Not only were Oliver's superiors and work col-leagues questioning whether they had promoted him prematurely but so was Oliver.

Oliver evaluated different leadership strategies that might help him resolve his problem. Among his options, Oliver considered whether he should stop getting too attached to his employees (become "Oliver the Machine"). This approach would allow him to handle his responsibilities with cold effi-ciency and avoid unnecessary emotions and stress. Firing someone would be a simple matter of numbers. The second option would be to increase his interactions with his employees with the aim of building positive relationships (become "Oliver the Idol"). This strategy is based on the idea that creating a flexible and engaging leadership structure would allow him to create a stress-free environment that would be beneficial to everybody. What's more, this approach would give him "permission" to fire those employees who exuded negativity. An alternative option would be to take a chance and create a spiritually minded work environment, promoting positivity and healing for workers (become "Oliver the Servant"). He could simply look at the firings as "meant to be for the greater good." If these approaches did not work, Oliver could choose to be an adaptive leader who deals with situations as they come (become "Oliver the Problem-Solver"). He could consider each employee's strength and weaknesses and, lacking sufficient differences, ultimately go with his gut to decide whom to terminate.

Which leadership strategy would you choose for Oliver to simultaneously improve his overall well-being and optimize organizational productivity?

Solving the Leadership Dilemma

Oliver's problem requires us to understand how human beings make decisions. As explained by Soosalu et al. in a study that references the robust body of research on this topic, human decision-making is oriented toward the intuitive (system 1) and the analytical (system 2) systems. System 1 encompasses instinctive decision-making such as "gut feeling," which is the faster mechanism. In comparison, system 2 consists of conscious, deliberate, and cognitive decision-making, which is obviously slower. In addition, system 1 is more susceptible to emotional and nonrational influences than system 2.[48] When people find themselves in a stressful situation, system 1 dominates system 2 and supports a flight-or-fight response.[49] The emotions and instincts that drive nonrational decision-making when in the fight-or-flight response are often fear-based and focused on surviving, rather than thriving.

There's no need to commit these systems to memory, as the conclusion is the same: rational and nonrational thought are separate decision-making entities. Simply keep in mind that the socialization state is where these decision-making processes integrate best. While some leaders may think that responding from a heightened mobilization state is how they "get things done," reacting from fear or anger to conquer an issue is not the same as responding wisely to a challenge. The key here is to find the sweet spot so that a leader can make optimal decisions even in the presence of adverse issues in the workplace, regardless of their leadership style. Let's turn to the Polyvagal Theory to see how it plays out in the four leadership approaches.

The Polyvagal Theory in Transactional Leadership

For many years, the transactional approach has been associated with rational decision-making. The transactional leadership style is highly structured, so it can provide important cues about danger and safety.

Although this leadership style is usually perceived to have an authoritarian style, it allows employees to gain a clear understanding of the leadership hierarchy.[50] The transactional leadership style also relies on rewards and punishments to encourage employees to improve productivity. As a result, this leadership style can easily increase stress and other adverse effects in the workplace because leaders prioritize their individualistic goals.[51] The reliance on rigid rules and guidelines can prevent the employees from developing social bonds, which are vital for reducing stress and other adverse influences in the workplace.

The high reliance on IQ allows transactional leaders to promote the distribution of tasks and rewards and build resilience against challenges. For "Oliver the Machine," the Polyvagal Theory explains that the leader is in the parasympathetic state at the top of the Polyvagal ladder—a perfect situation where rational and nonrational decision-making is at its peak. In this state, the leader has the ability to make good rational decisions without being affected by negative and emotional practices. Even in the sympathetic state, the employees will have their own attitudes and domain-specific behaviors to ensure they develop properly.[52] In addition, it is essential to mention that transactional leadership allows leaders to monitor their subordinates' behavior in order to determine when positive correction can be provided to improve the employees' outcomes.[53] In brief, transactional leadership promotes calmness even when employees transition from the parasympathetic state to the less intense degrees of the sympathetic state, though transactional leadership is more task-focused than relationship-oriented.

Effective Application of the Polyvagal Theory in Transactional Leadership

Given the challenges that Oliver has been dealing with since his promotion, he has decided to select the transactional approach, which emphasizes authoritative and rational decision-making. The transactional approach will allow him to deal with professional responsibilities efficiently. From this perspective, the best way to motivate his employees is to use appropriate rewards and punishments. He insists that good employees will receive flexible work schedules or free subscriptions to luxury facilities, such as gyms and restaurants. However, low-performing workers will receive simple punishments, such as being the ones chosen to cover the office on holidays. He understands that everyone in the department dislikes performance reviews because consistently poor reviews may cause them to be laid off. Instead of placing too much emphasis on how the employees view him, Oliver's objective is to build a reputation of being a fair boss at all times. This approach typically causes employees to shift between the sympathetic and parasympathetic states, depending on whether they are entitled to rewards or punishments. However, this approach will allow him to gain comprehensive insights into the employees' motivations and resilience. Building instinctive leadership traits will play a vital role in enhancing Oliver's decision-making in accordance with his employees' motivations. Oliver's goal is to create a mutually beneficial professional relationship with his employees that improves the department's productivity.

Polyvagal Theory in Transformational Leadership

The transformational leadership style is associated with the socialization state. In this state, the person requires both analytical and instinctive decision-making to determine their interactions with other staff. Research shows that leaders who favor the transactional leadership style usually focus on *idiocentric* followers, employees who prefer individualistic orientations.[54] In comparison, the transformational style is usually adopted to manage *allocentric* followers, employees who prioritize the well-being of others. This rationale explains why transformational leadership places emphasis on social engagement and mutual collaboration. Nonetheless, the main challenge facing this leadership approach lies in the lack of clarity regarding its objectives and outcomes.[55] Therefore, the transformational approach is relatively popular, but it has several weaknesses that hinder its implementation in real-life settings.

While rational decision-making is usually considered an important consideration in transactional leadership, the transformational leadership style combines rational and nonrational decision-making. Harms et al. explain that the transformational leadership style is perceived to offer "psychological comfort" during times of uncertainty.[56] In addition, the leadership approach promotes resilience, optimism, and self-efficacy in the organizational environment. Therefore, research highlights that transformational leadership is dependent on leaders' ability to lead from the front and their competency when addressing the staff's emotional needs.

Reliable research finds that transformational leadership is associated with a reduction in stress and other adverse emotions by building a positive work environment for workers. Transformational leadership also encourages self-regulation, thereby encouraging workers to control their actions and thoughts, even when they experience threats.[57] While the transactional approach may easily push the employee from the parasympathetic to the sympathetic state, the transformational approach is more attuned to creating cues of safety that encourage employees to open up. In brief, socialization is a vital component of transformational leadership. Team members see themselves as part of a larger group, with an emphasis on supporting each other in achieving mutual goals.

Effective Application of the Polyvagal Theory in Transformational Leadership

Oliver hopes his transformational leadership approach will allow him to create a positive work environment that strengthens social engagement and collaboration between him and his staff. He recognized the importance of understanding his employees' opinions, motivations, and ambitions through social engagement. This leadership strategy also compels him to provide freedom and autonomy to his employees. He believes this method will allow him to understand the challenges that prevent employees from delivering optimal productivity. He aspires to provide psychological and emotional comfort to his workers in a manner that will encourage them to improve their overall productivity. Through this strategy, Oliver feels he will gain a proper understanding of his workers to the extent of making instinctive decisions simply based on his "gut" perceptions of his workers. Therefore, the transformational leadership style will allow him to create a conducive atmosphere by appealing to their social engagement systems.

Polyvagal Theory in Servant Leadership

Servant leadership differs from the transactional and transformational leadership styles because it focuses on stimulating the growth of the team by promoting morality and ethical behaviors in the workplace. Accordingly, servant leadership is similar to transformational leadership because it also relies on social engagement and the socialization dimension of the Polyvagal Theory to inform decision-making. In modern organizations, however, most prefer leadership structures that are politically oriented rather than spiritually oriented.[58] This problem often manifests because politically oriented leadership structures are usually aligned with rules and guidelines.[59] In comparison, spirituality is a nonrational aspect of human decision-making. However, servant leadership is unique because it places emphasis on using spirituality and morality to create a positive work environment.

In the sympathetic state, workers often experience adverse mental and emotional influences that can skew decision-making. Accordingly, servant leadership relies on emotional healing to improve the physical, mental, and emotional well-being of employees.[60] Simple actions such as empathizing with the employees and listening to their pains and aspirations can promote recovery. Through compassion, leaders can gain important insights into their employees' social, emotional, financial, and administrative well-being. Therefore, researchers highlight that the servant leadership approach places significant weight on the autonomic processing of information instead of rational processing.[61] This method allows the servant leader to resolve stress and trauma in the workplace. In brief, the Polyvagal Theory highlights that nonrational decision-making is an integral dimension in servant leadership that encourages leaders to focus on their workers' well-being, especially when they transition from the parasympathetic to the sympathetic state. This approach is more focused on the leader helping the individual team member, rather than on the whole group, and thus is less associated with a high degree of socialization.

Effective Application of the Polyvagal Theory in Servant Leadership

Oliver's servant leadership approach allows him to prioritize the employees' needs instead of continually focusing on the department's objectives. Oliver believes that the department's problems cannot be resolved through conventional human resource strategies. Accordingly, the servant leadership style places emphasis on the socialization state through the creation of a spiritual environment. From Oliver's perspective, this strategy will allow him to make major changes to his department. Foremost, he will create a peaceful environment that will improve the staff's mental and emotional well-being. In addition, he hopes to grasp his employees' strengths and weaknesses to better understand how he can nurture them to strengthen the department's overall productivity. Although servant leadership requires him to dedicate a lot of time and effort to understanding his employees, none of the leadership strategies can offer him the same level of understanding of his staff's strengths and weaknesses. Therefore, Oliver perceives servant leadership as the most effective style for enhancing social engagement in his department.

Polyvagal Theory in Situational Leadership

Situational leadership is aligned with nurturing the right cognitive mechanisms for solving organizational issues through socialization. In current times, most organizations experience complex situations that compel leaders to make major decisions using rational and nonrational methods. Common workplace crises include work overload, burnout, low performance, bullying, and other problems. In such cases, leaders are encouraged to rely on approaches that are explicitly designed to address organizational problems.[62] The transactional style is not appropriate in such scenarios because the leaders do not highlight the need to receive input from subordinates. Similarly, the transformational style is not suitable for such problems because it is often hampered by unclear goals and objectives.[63] Thus, during times of stress, the situational leadership style offers the right balance of analytical and instinctive decision-making.

Considering the challenges of maintaining employee satisfaction and motivation in the modern workplace, leaders can gain multiple benefits by merging the analytical and instinctive cognitive mechanisms. The analytical component can encourage the workers to focus on how situational leadership improves performance and work quality.[64] In comparison, the instinctive aspect is oriented toward managing employee relationships and interactions. The underlying rationale for this mechanism is that every problem has different characteristics, so they require solutions that are tailored to address the problem.[65] Organizational behavior is strongly dependent on the leaders' actions and their ability to transfer essential knowledge and skills to workers during different scenarios. Situational leadership is particularly important during times of stress and uncertainty because it communicates the leader's crisis-solving capabilities.[66] For that reason, Balasubramanian and Fernandes published a study that claimed that situational leadership was the most effective strategy for handling emerging crises, such as the start of the global pandemic in early 2020.[67] Hence, situational leadership tends to deliver positive results through analytical and instinctive decision-making, regardless of the overall state of the nervous system.

Effective Application of the Polyvagal Theory in Situational Leadership

Oliver recognizes that he needs to utilize flexible and adaptive methods to resolve the human resource challenges in his department. The situational leadership style requires a unique balance between rational and nonrational decision-making to ensure one is able to deal with emerging organizational challenges. From Oliver's perspective, the best approach is to respond to situations as they emerge. As a result, the situational leadership strategy is more suitable for cultivating instinctive leadership. In the workplace, it is inevitable that one will face unexpected challenges on a regular basis. Accordingly, the leader's response to the challenges will reveal their level of competence and their problem-solving capabilities. In his department, Oliver believes that the best employees will reveal themselves based on their foresight. He aims to build a workforce that can identify problems and resolve them as soon as they emerge. Although he understands that he will face many challenges before he builds the appropriate levels of instinctive leadership, he knows that situational leadership will allow him to create a strong and resilient workforce that can make both analytical and instinctive decisions. In summary, it can be perceived that situational leadership can allow him to navigate through both the sympathetic and parasympathetic states.

While we have been making a case for situational leadership with an emphasis on integrated decision-making, the leadership strategy a leader adopts should take all factors into consideration, including the corporate culture, the position, the role of the subordinates, and more. For example, a certain field or department may require more structure than others, leaving little room for creative input from employees, but other professions or job functions may rely entirely on innovation. For some teams, structure and clearly delineated expectations keep them feeling safe, whereas others need more flexibility and freedom to remain in the socialization state.

KEY POINTS

- A leader's decision-making mechanisms become skewed when the fight-or-flight response is activated, regardless of leadership style.
- Although it is important to focus on the internal and external organizational influences that affect decisions in the workplace, it is also vital to analyze how the state of the autonomic nervous systems affects both the leader and their staff to improve outcomes.
- An instinctive leader has the ability to make choices based on comprehensive analytical processes while also integrating intuitive aspects into their decisions.
- Organizations need to develop strategies that nurture rational and nonrational decision-making in the workplace in order to develop leaders who can make optimal decisions regardless of the challenges they face.

CHAPTER 3

Recruiting and Retaining Your Staff

N ow that we've explored the application of the Polyvagal Theory in various leadership styles, we'll turn our focus to the recruitment and selection processes and the underlying biases that prevent leaders from recruiting the *right* workers. Consequently, we'll explain how a balance of rational and nonrational decision-making can be achieved considering the three states outlined by the Polyvagal Theory: (1) socialization, (2) mobilization, and (3) immobilization. After a brief visit from Oliver Green, we'll look at the main factors that should be considered when selecting candidates. Then, we'll clarify how leaders can create organizational cultures that contain less drama, stress, and trauma. It's our hope that you'll come away from this chapter with a better pulse on how to cultivate a more secure and productive staff.

Is Oliver Green Biased?

Oliver's seemingly insurmountable challenges in his new role as senior executive have increased his stress levels, resulting in moodiness and irritably. Currently, his main priority is to recruit and select a candidate to fill his previous position. Being intimately familiar with the responsibilities of the role, Oliver is sure he can find someone to fill the position quickly. He tells himself it will be a piece of cake. The best candidate will share certain key characteristics with him and will also be good at stock trading as well as human resource management. However, Oliver later realizes that it's more challenging than he thought. The job requires someone who is both decisive and resilient. They'll need to know when to "cut losses" but should also be able to persevere through daily challenges.

Three weeks into a recruitment process that was supposed to be completed within two weeks, Oliver has still not found the right person for the job. His colleagues have begun questioning why the department still has a vacancy after so many qualified recruits have been interviewed. Oliver evaluates his requirements: *Are they too high? Am I being unrealistic?* He looks back at his reasons for eliminating applicants: "He seems too slow," "That one wasn't decisive enough," "She doesn't have enough experience talking to customers," "I don't think he has the instinct for it," and "With a three-month-old baby at home, she won't be able to dedicate enough time to work."

After a short reflection, Oliver calls back the best candidates and decides to use a structured checklist to evaluate the applicants' competencies. Surely, he knows this method will allow him to find at least *one* good candidate among them.

Was Oliver truly unable to identify a suitable candidate for the position, or did he use biased reasons for eliminating the applicants?

Organizational Recruitment and Selection Process

To understand how the Polyvagal Theory can be applied to Oliver's issue to find a solution, let's consider the conventional organization recruitment and selection process. The main stages of recruitment and selection are prescreening, recruitment, and selection.

Research shows that bias in the talent acquisition process often emerges because of poor performance and selection methods.[1] Fundamentally, most recruiters use methods that are tailored to the recruitment goals and the target applicants. However, due to the complexity of the objectives and methods, organizational recruitment and selection can be quite challenging. What's more, as in Oliver's case, bias can emerge at different stages of the process, which can become even more pronounced under unchecked stress, when the recruiter is caught in the sympathetic state, thereby affecting the reliability of nonrational thinking.

In the prescreening stage, bias often occurs when job-irrelevant considerations such as demographic, personal, or organizational factors sway the recruiter's employment decisions.[2] In the recruitment stage, bias tends to emerge when the recruiter uses methods that are partial toward specific groups. For example, posting a job ad on a social media site frequented only by the youngest generation may not be seen by older candidates who have more experience and expertise. The selection stage involves the use of different mechanisms to cross-examine and identify suitable candidates through interviews, psychometric assessments, and assessment centers.[3] When candidates are independently assessed using a wide range of selection exercises, bias generally plays less of a role at this stage, but this isn't the case for all organizations. There's still an opportunity for a recruiter to be swayed by their judgments and biases.

How Stress Worsens Bias and Discrimination in Recruitment and Selection

In the case of Oliver Green, he had initially rejected all the applicants, even those who had high academic and professional qualifications, for a variety of biased reasons. His colleagues were flabbergasted, which shot his stress levels even higher. Oliver believed he had two choices: sacrifice his personal opinions and offer the job to anyone who meets the prerequisites or abandon the recruitment and selection process because it would be pointless to recruit someone he perceives as incompetent. Oliver's stress level skewed his decision-making ability.

Bias is unfortunately quite common in the modern organizational environment, and it transpires in both implicit and explicit ways. For example, Oliver's bias against the new mother was explicit, while his bias against the others was implicit. Explicit bias is associated with evident forms of bias due to reasons such as in-group distrust, fear, discomfort, ignorance, or false perceptions.[4] It is easier to address explicit bias because it manifests in obvious ways. Implicit bias occurs when a person makes unconscious mental associations due to a lack of control, underlying social perceptions, or personal impressions, making it more difficult to address.[5]

For this discussion, be aware that most of our behavior, thoughts, and actions largely depend on the state of the body and what it is communicating to the brain. As you now understand, stressful and traumatic circumstances can cause a person to shift from one autonomic state to another, or down the Polyvagal Ladder—from socialization to mobilization to immobilization. The ideal position from which to recruit a new worker is obviously socialization.

Research shows that stress and trauma can impact the recruitment and selection process. For instance, studies published following the 2020 pandemic revealed that stress negatively affected talent acquisition. Maurer explains that stress levels among organizational recruiters increased by approximately 61 percent for reasons that included difficulty shifting from face-to-face practices to digital work strategies.[6] When stress triggers the body to shift from the parasympathetic state to the sympathetic state, these emotional influences can cause profound changes in the recruiters' behaviors and decision-making, thereby increasing bias and discrimination.

With regard to trauma, this emotional response is usually associated with immobilization. Nonetheless, there are severe gaps in existing literature regarding trauma in the workplace and the development of a trauma-informed workforce.[7] Research shows that trauma can easily lead to distorted decision-making, poor concentration, anxiety, social withdrawal, and restlessness. In extreme situations, it can cause the body to become immobilized. Unlike typical animals, the autonomic response in human beings does not allow them to maintain high decision-making capabilities when they experience trauma. While typical animals can quickly return to the standard mode of function once the traumatic incident has passed, human beings lack this capability, causing many to find themselves trapped in a recurring trauma response well after the traumatic event is over.[8] Therefore, targeted interventions are required to ensure that the decisions of organizational leaders are not negatively affected by the trauma response. A full discussion of trauma in the workplace goes beyond the scope of this book, but an awareness of its potential impact, including worsening bias and discrimination, is essential.

Most organizations do attempt to mitigate bias and discrimination through comprehensive recruitment and selection structures,[9] but it is still quite difficult to curb implicit forms of bias, especially during traumatic and/or stressful times. Some examples of explicit bias include statements like, "She can't handle the job *and* care for a new baby," "People from his culture are known for being highly intelligent," and "That person is too old; the job will be more than they can handle." These comments reflect situations where the recruiter showed explicit bias due to the candidates' sex, race, and age. In comparison, implicit forms of bias are less evident. For example, "I like that person's name; he seems like a strong candidate,"

"I'm not sure about hiring that kind of person," and "You can see that he is a bad fit for the company." These implicit forms of bias cannot be easily identified without a clear understanding of the recruiter's intentions.

Overall, the differences between implicit and explicit bias are dependent on a person's intentions and psychological state. When a person transitions from the parasympathetic state to the sympathetic state, they are less able to check themselves for biases, as they are now more prone to make impulsive choices. Those who are on the receiving end of perceived biases are more likely to shift down the ladder as well, as their body mobilizes necessary resources by triggering the sympathetic nervous system.[10]

Table 3.1 outlines the main types of implicit bias that emerge during recruitment and selection. Leaders need to adopt interventions, which first includes learning about and identifying each bias and form of discrimination, to overcome them. Again, we make an example of overwhelmed Oliver Green to bring to light how many forms of bias and discrimination can be uncovered.

Table 3.1 Bias and Discrimination in Recruitment and Selection

Bias/Discrimination	Description	Examples
Selective attention	Occurs when the interview focuses on specific aspects of the applicants. For instance, disregarding information that does not meet the expected criteria.	Oliver has been rejecting applicants because he has been placing too much attention on two specific traits: resiliency and decisiveness.
In-group bias	Emerges when the recruiter believes they have a special affinity with applicants from specific groups. For example, seeking candidates who share similar traits, skills, beliefs, and life pursuits.	Oliver wants to hire someone who shares similar characteristics with him because he feels the employee will need those characteristics to fulfill the duties of the job.

(continued)

Table 3.1 Bias and Discrimination in Recruitment and Selection *(continued)*

Bias/Discrimination	Description	Examples
Overconfidence bias	Manifests when the recruiter is too confident in their ability to identify suitable candidates. Intuition is highlighted as the main consideration associated with this bias.	Oliver has too much confidence in his analytical skills and his personal perceptions. This problem caused him to overlook many candidates with high potential.
Appraisal bias	Transpires when the recruiter provides lower scores to people from minority groups than their performance deserves. In other words, the use of subjective criteria instead of objective ones.	Oliver has been assigning lower scores to workers from specific minority groups. For instance, the belief that women with newborn babies lack commitment for work.
Attributional bias	Occurs when the recruiter assumes there is a causal relationship between an unrelated factor and the applicant's ability to perform.	Oliver has made many wrong assumptions about the candidates based on attributes he identified. For example, one candidate spoke slowly, which Oliver believed implied he'd be slow at the job.
First-impression bias	Emerges when the recruiter develops assumptions based on their initial interactions with the candidate and assumes a candidate lacks a necessary quality as a result of their first conversation.	Oliver eliminated many applicants based on his first impressions of them for a variety of reasons, including their looks, style of dress, affectations, and body language.
Confirmation bias	Ensues when the recruiter accepts information that is associated with their perceived expectations. For example, interpreting information in a way that confirms one's experiences or beliefs.	Oliver interpreted the results in a manner that allowed him to make clear-cut decisions about the applicants. If he had used different methods (e.g., scorecard), he would have acquired different results.
Conformity bias	Occurs when the recruiter makes a conclusion based on the influence of peers and colleagues. This bias tends to subconsciously change the recruiter's perceptions in accordance with popular opinions.	Oliver's methods were designed with his *own* interests in mind to acquire an employee who possessed specific desirable characteristics, so he was not subject to conformity bias.
Halo effect	This bias occurs when the recruiter believes that the applicant's skills and competencies are complementary. In other words, excelling in one area implies the candidate is talented in related areas.	Oliver didn't have this issue, as none of the applicants stood out enough for him to make such assumptions.
Horn effect	Occurs in opposition to the Halo effect, whereby the recruiter assumes that low performance in one area reflects their incompetency in others.	Oliver believed the job position required clear strength in several areas, so he didn't bother asking further questions if the candidate showed potential weakness in one of those areas.

(continued)

Table 3.1 Bias and Discrimination in Recruitment and Selection *(continued)*

Bias/Discrimination	Description	Examples
Expectation anchor	Emerges when the recruiter narrows down the application process toward specific characteristics. For instance, claiming that all applicants should be both social and decisive.	Oliver placed too much emphasis on specific characteristics he believed would allow him to identify the right candidates.
Taste-based discrimination	This bias occurs when the employer develops preferences aligned with specific applicant characteristics: physique, race, nationality, or sexual orientation.	This bias emerged because Oliver relied on his personal preferences to judge the participants instead of structured, bias-immune methods.
Statistical discrimination	Manifests when the organization uses statistical criteria to justify false perceptions about the recruitment process. The statistics can reveal that certain population groups are not suitable for filling a vacant position.	This bias was not evident in Oliver's case because he didn't rely on statistical methods to evaluate the employee's qualification.

VanderPal, G., and R. Brazie, Exploratory Study of Polyvagal Theory and Underlying Stress and Trauma That Influence Major Leadership Approaches, *Journal of Applied Business and Economics* 24, no. (2022).

Oliver's decisions were affected by several biases, and while he is usually an upstanding guy, he was clearly operating outside his comfort zone in a state of high stress. Among the biases listed in Table 3.1, the most evident in Oliver's case are expectation bias and first-impression bias. These forms of discrimination encompass a large majority of the mistakes he made during employee recruitment. When he returned to the sympathetic state, Oliver was painfully aware that he had succumbed to these biases. He recognized that the daily challenges he faced at work had compelled him to shift to (and remain in) the mobilization state, causing him to rely even more on his biases and preconceived notions. What's more, at some point in the recruitment process, he became immobilized, ready to admit defeat and abandon the process altogether. It was a painful lesson, but Oliver was starting to develop a better understanding of himself and planned to make a sincere effort toward returning to the top of the Polyvagal Ladder and remaining there as often as possible and ensuring that his team members do as well.

Developing a More Effective Workforce

To be effective at creating high-performing teams, leaders as well as any member involved in recruitment need to develop an instinctive understanding of themselves and their surroundings. When necessary, they need to be able to shift from "I can't" (immbolization) to "I can" (mobilization) and "I am" (see Figure 3.1). The same is true for the people they lead. Interestingly, research shows that just the act of labeling the autonomic responses can influence behavioral outcomes and improve vagal nerve functions.[11] So, being able to identify these states in oneself is an excellent step toward good decision-making and increased productivity. While you may be surprised, based on our discussion thus far, that the mobilization state is described as an "I can" state rather than an "I must" state, be aware that there's a distinct line between being mobilized to do something as a result of an event or a need and being mobilized by fear or anger. Remember, although we aren't going too deeply into the subtle differences that change as the level of intensity increases or decreases, the process of moving up and down the Polyvagal Ladder is not necessarily a huge leap from one state to the next.

In the parasympathetic dorsal vagal state, the recruiter is immobilized, which makes decision-making difficult. Shifting to the sympathetic state tends to encourage the recruiter to succumb to the fight-or-flight response, but

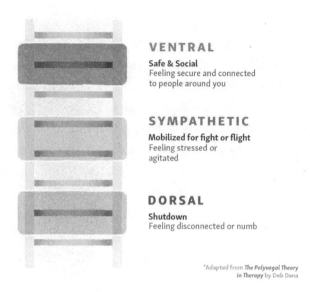

VENTRAL

Safe & Social
Feeling secure and connected
to people around you

SYMPATHETIC

Mobilized for fight or flight
Feeling stressed or
agitated

DORSAL

Shutdown
Feeling disconnected or numb

*Adapted from *The Polyvagal Theory
in Therapy* by Deb Dana

Figure 3.1 Personal Perception in the Polyvagal States

Source: *Redeemer Counseling* (blog). (n.d.). Redeemer Counseling. https://www
.redeemercounselingcenter.com/articles

with an awareness of this shift, the recruiter can recalibrate. For Oliver to become more effective, he needs to figure out how to achieve balance to be able to rely on rational and nonrational decision-making in a manner that prevents him from resorting to bias or discrimination. Let's consider five of the most feasible recommendations for Oliver regarding how to be a more effective leader in general but also how to be more adept at recruitment.

Match an Employee's Baseline Autonomic State to the Position

Oliver needs to understand that the three autonomic states reflect three organizational positions: leaders, frontline workers, and back-end workers. Foremost, the leaders are expected to make optimal decisions in the calm state, so this position matches the socialization stage of the Polyvagal Ladder. Leaders are the backbone of the organization, so their choices need to be effective. Consequently, frontline workers often handle interactions with different organizational stakeholders, such as customers, workers, and other personnel. These workers deal with conflict on a frequent basis. For that reason, these workers are often exposed to moments of stress and anxiety that drive them to the mobilization stage. Frontline workers are usually resilient due to their ability to cope with excessive stress and anxiety levels with different workers. With regard to back-end workers, these employees usually handle support roles in the organization. Back-end workers lack the same resilience as frontline workers, so moments of extreme stress or fear tend to easily push them to the immobilization state.

To improve the department's performance and select the right candidates, Oliver needs to ensure that an employee's baseline autonomic state is suitable for the position. (See "What's a Baseline Autonomic State?" at the end of this section.) This understanding will give him the ability to better match candidates to appropriate roles. Being aware of the three states of the Polyvagal Ladder—socialization, mobilization, and immobilization—helps the recruiter recognize whether the applicant has the basic prerequisites for a specific position.

Let's further break down the three organizational positions as they relate to their classifications on the Polyvagal Ladder. In the first category, someone who exhibits the socialization state is usually characterized by strong social engagement tendencies. Such people can deliver high performance when they are engaged and committed in their respective positions. For instance, a salesperson typically embodies the socialization state. Employees who have these characteristics tend to have high social and communication abilities, which allow them to have positive interactions with customers and other personnel. Applicants characterized by high socialization are also suitable candidates for leadership roles because their actions and decisions are not as influenced by the sympathetic state.

In comparison, an applicant in the mobilization state is likely to experience repetitive shifts from the socialization state to the mobilization state. In other words, these individuals usually have a high disposition toward the flight-or-flight response. As a result, they may display some nervousness or anxiety. In some cases, they may talk fast, get distracted easily, or seem impatient. This does not mean that being in the mobilization state implies the worker is a low performer. A suitable example of an employee in the mobilization state is a customer care worker. Compared to the salesperson, who has more control over whom they interact with, the customer care assistant usually faces more challenges. Customer care workers often experience numerous challenges in their professions: dealing with rude and aggressive customers, handling work roles that were not specified in their job descriptions, and dealing with high workloads. As a result, it can be perceived that the customer care worker will deal with more stress than the salesperson. Such workers can deliver high performance even when they are placed in fast-paced positions, but they may also lose attention or get bored too quickly. These workers are generally not suited for roles involving more tedious or repetitive tasks.

A person in a state of immobilization is usually characterized by low energy states and functions when compared to applicants in the socialization or mobilization states. These people often perform better in slow-paced work environments that require minimal engagement with others. Furthermore, these workers may prefer structured professional roles. Workers in these roles are often associated with back-office positions such as accounting. The accounting position is relatively calm when compared to sales or customer care. Accountants handle various activities with minimal engagement. Thus, a person whose baseline is the immobilization state may struggle to work in collaborative environments while demonstrating outstanding performance in individual settings. These workers are generally not suitable for leadership positions.

Oliver can use this information to determine which candidate suits the job description best. He currently relies on vague recruitment and selection criteria that are highly vulnerable to bias and discrimination. Therefore, the best recommendation is for him to identify how a vacant job position relates to the applicant's baseline autonomic state.

What's a Baseline Autonomic State?

We've been discussing at length how stress and trauma compel our bodies to move down the Polyvagal Ladder—from socialization to mobilization to immobilization. What's also true is that each person naturally spends most of their time in one of these three states, which is referred to as a baseline autonomic state. You may know of someone who tends to be fidgety, restless, and somewhat hyperactive. This person tends to remain in the sympathetic area. In contrast, you may recall someone who tends to speak softly and is more laid-back, slower to act, and less active. This person may predominantly remain in a dorsal vagal parasympathetic state. And, finally, think of someone who is very sociable but also calm—this person may reside largely in a ventral vagal state of social engagement.

Regardless of the baseline autonomic state, shifting from one state to another is still part of everyday life; it's just that each person tends to return to their baseline state. It's important to mention here that this baseline state *can* be shifted with polyvagal-informed therapy and practices, discussed later. That aside, like a baseline state, each person has their own level of tolerance before they are triggered to descend further down the ladder. This is called the "window of tolerance," and we'll revisit this concept later.

Create an Accurate Job Description

It's essential to create an accurate job description that highlights the position and expected qualities of the applicant. In Oliver's case, he lacked a clear benchmark for evaluating the applicants. As a result, his subconscious drove him to reject candidates who did not portray the expected qualities. This approach is flawed because there is no practical method for evaluating an absent construct. For instance, if Oliver wanted to recruit risk-takers, he should have outlined in the job advertisement that the job requires risk-taking. As a result, the candidates are unlikely to portray their risk-taking capabilities to the full extent. Accurate job descriptions are essential not only for guiding applicants but also for clarifying the recruitment and selection criteria. Another benefit of this approach is that it can eliminate implicit or explicit bias in the company's talent acquisition process.

This recommendation goes beyond merely identifying the key roles and responsibilities of the job vacancy.

Recruiters must analyze how the respective job position ranks among the three autonomic states. As a result, the recruiters will also develop mechanisms for discerning when they develop bias or discrimination toward specific candidates. In *Polyvagal Exercises for Safety and Connection*, Deb Dana recommends the use of a "personal profile map" to understand the physiological and psychological traits of workers.[12] A personal profile map can offer guidance into the participant's perceptions to the wordless experience of neuroception. In this context, these traits are summarized using the label "character," and the job positions are classified in accordance with the autonomic states on the Polyvagal Ladder. Let's look at how this plays out using the job descriptions that are aligned with these states: leaders, frontline workers, and back-office workers.

Foremost, the leader is expected to make decisions in a calm and composed manner. For that reason, the job description for such positions demands applicants who exemplify the socialization characteristic. The ventral vagal complex (VVC) component of the Polyvagal Theory supports social engagement when the body receives stimuli indicating that the environment is safe.[13] Accordingly, the VVC can enhance communication, listening ability, and vocalization, thereby providing more opportunities for optimizing social interactions.[14] These characteristics are essential among leaders, who often handle multiple responsibilities and stressful situations daily.

Research by Seijts and Gandz supports that good character is integral for effective leadership. The researchers identified 11 key dimensions of leader character that can enhance leadership skills: drive, collaboration, humanity, humility, integrity, temperance, justice, accountability, courage, transcendence, and judgment.[15] Figure 3.2 highlights the relative importance of each character in the organizational setting. Therefore, recruiters need to highlight these characteristics to ensure the recruitment and selection of candidates who have both the credentials and the character for good organizational leadership.

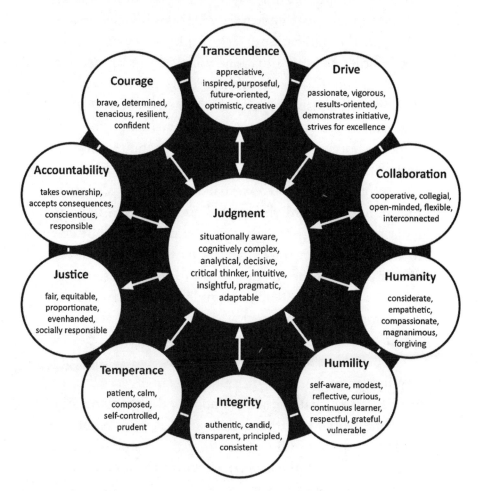

Figure 3.2 Characteristics That Define Good Leaders

Source: Seijts, G.H., & Gandz, J. (2017). Transformational change and leader character, *Business Horizons 61*(2), 239–249.

In comparison, frontline workers are usually expected to make decisions in both conducive and unconducive work environments. Consequently, these workers have considerable experience making quick decisions in emergency situations. While the VVC is linked to social engagement, the sympathetic nervous system (SNS) is oriented toward dealing with behaviors and emotions related to anger, fear, and anxiety.[16] This rationale explains why most organizations seek frontline workers who can handle stressful situations with a positive attitude. Research shows that frontline workers often experience situations of abusive supervision and customer incivility that lead to stress and emotional exhaustion.[17] For such frontline occupations, organizations require workers with resilient characters in order to mitigate the adverse effects of internal and external stressors, as shown in Figure 3.3. By highlighting resilience as a vital requirement in job advertisements, the organization will be able to analyze whether the employees have "what it takes" to handle frontline occupational roles for prolonged periods. However, it is essential to understand that resilience is an important resource that can be depleted with frequent and continuous exposure to stressors.[18] Figure 3.2 illustrates that leadership in the socialization state requires a combination of multiple traits, while Figure 3.3 illustrates that the most important characteristic of frontline workers in the mobilization state is employee resilience. These findings highlight that employee resilience can mediate the adverse effects of the mobilization state among frontline workers.

The final autonomic state reflects the job characteristics of back-office workers. As mentioned earlier, individuals with an autonomic baseline of immobilization

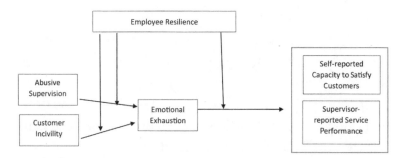

Figure 3.3 Importance of Resilience for Frontline Workers in the Mobilization State

Source: Al-Hawari, M.A., Bani-Melhem, S., & Quratulain, S. (2020). Do frontline employees cope effectively with abusive supervision and customer incivility? Testing the effect of employee resilience, *Journal of Business and Psychology 35*, 223–240.

are usually characterized by low energy states and functions, as well as a proclivity for slow-paced job interactions. In these workers, the dorsal vagal complex (DVC) *often* triggers the immobilization state when the person experiences situations of extreme stress, danger, or terror.[19] Keep in mind, however, that their perception of *extreme* stress, danger, or terror may not seem so extreme to others. That's why workers who are highly suscepti- ble to the immobilization state are suited for back-office positions. These employees are usually separated from customers, so they remain largely invisible to many orga- nizational stakeholders.[20] The purpose of transferring these workers to back-office roles is to reduce the expo- sure of these workers to internal and external stressors. While frontline workers are expected to deal with mul- tiple stressors daily, back-office workers are more suited for safe environments to reduce the adverse impacts of the immobilization state on their physical, emotional, and mental well-being. Such situations may require active avoidance or passive avoidance.[21] For that reason, researchers highlight emotional intelligence as an important trait of back-office workers that allows them to accurately analyze and understand the feelings of other workers in the surrounding environment.[22] In addition, high emotional intelligence can allow the workers to dedicate adequate attention to their roles instead of constantly experiencing the freezing state.

Identify Applicant Groups Affected by Bias and Discrimination

As illustrated, Oliver is biased toward certain applicant groups. For example, he feels that the vacant position is not suitable for women with young children or elderly workers. To address this issue, Oliver needs to acknowledge that his decisions are either implicitly or explicitly biased. By recognizing the problem, Oliver will reduce the subconscious influences that drive him to label certain people as unfit candidates. In brief, Oliver needs to gain control of his nonrational mental faculties to eliminate bias in his decision-making.

Research shows that there are certain job applicant groups that increase the probability of bias and discrimination. For instance, ethnicity, gender, age, socioeconomic status, and disability are the main dimensions of discrimination in the organizational context. These categories are the root causes of implicit and explicit bias in the recruitment and selection process. With regard to ethnicity, researchers show that many recruiters evaluate applicants based on their ethnic backgrounds. Berry and Bell (2012) explain that some recruiters place too much focus on the "whiteness" or "blackness" of the applicant's name, thereby approving applicants with white-sounding names.[23] Although many modern organizations have attempted to mitigate ethnic discrimination, the reality is that this form of prejudice has just become more implicit.

With regard to gender, research shows that gender discrimination affects both men and women, but female workers are the most frequent targets of discrimination.[24] For example, women are often rejected during job applications or assigned to low-paying positions due to the perception that their professions are more suited for men. In addition, members of the LGBTQ community face more severe forms of discrimination compared to heterosexual individuals due to their unique gender identities or sexual orientations.[25] In such cases, the main responses to explicit bias are administrative or legal action. However, it is important to consider alternative solutions for dealing with implicit bias that addresses implicit discrimination. Thus, acknowledging that gender is a major cause of bias can alleviate its occurrence in recruitment and selection processes.

Research also shows that socioeconomic status is a major cause of bias among recruiters. For example, some recruiters subconsciously believe that employees with low socioeconomic status results in workers with higher job insecurity.[26] In many cases, socioeconomic status is aligned with the workers' education status or their financial well-being.[27] As a result, many organizations have a tendency to assign workers with low socioeconomic status to low-paying jobs or to occupations that involve high physical risks. In other cases, these applicants may face more challenges finding appropriate job opportunities than candidates with high socioeconomic status. It should be clear that organizations need to move away from socioeconomic status by prioritizing the applicants' capabilities, character, and work experience.

The final two categories are age and disability status. These two categories are usually aligned with explicit forms of bias. In the modern organizational environment, most corporations prefer applicants who deliver maximum input to organizational activities. This practice adversely affects the recruitment of older or disabled applicants due to their individual limitations. For older workers, research shows that a vast majority of workers over 45 years old experience discrimination in the workplace.[28] Workers who have reached their senior years may be denied promotions, laid off, or excluded from employee training opportunities. With regard to disabled applicants, these candidates usually suffer from similar situations as the senior population due to their limited capacities. Disabled workers are often restricted from working in certain occupational positions or may be retrenched due to their disabilities.[29] Although various legislation has been implemented to protect these people, these measures are inadequate for mitigating hidden forms of discrimination.

There are two approaches for addressing the mentioned types of discrimination in the organizational setting. The Polyvagal Theory can be applied to mediate the influences that cause bias and discrimination by recognizing how these factors shape a person's worldly perceptions. With that said, the first approach for mediating the influences is to promote employee diversity during recruitment and selection. Diversity and inclusion can improve equality in accordance with the applicants' background, gender, age, sexual orientation, ethnicity, religion, culture, disability, or socioeconomic status. Accordingly, research shows that organizations that embrace the diversity of different groups can improve their problem-solving and innovation capabilities.[30] Diversity and inclusion can be achieved by ensuring adequate representation of different applicant groups in the recruitment and selection process.

The second approach for addressing discrimination requires recruiters to shift the focus from the applicants' individual differences to instead prioritize job-related factors. While the first approach promotes diversity and inclusion, the second approach places more focus on eliminating discrimination by giving precedence to the applicants' competencies rather than to their differences. For instance, the use of "blind screening" methods during the review of applicant CVs or résumés can allow the recruiters to create a neutral talent acquisition process.[31] Another strategy in this approach is to use artificial intelligence technologies as part of the process to conduct recruitment and selection.[32] An AI system can be programmed to identify and analyze for important experience and hiring attributes without human filtering. It's important to mention here that selection bias may not just be based on gender, religion, age, or origin; it can also include factors such as clothing style, tone of voice, and facial expressions that may endear or disengage the interviewer.

Create a Corporate Culture with Less Drama, Stress, and Trauma

Another way to improve organizational staffing is to create a conducive work environment with minimal drama, stress, and trauma. Oliver's work environment and conditions increase his susceptibility to bias and discrimination. In the socialization state, he is capable of making effective decisions that emphasize his leadership and decision-making skills. However, moments of extreme stress and trauma tend to drive him to make poor choices. To address this problem, Oliver needs to create a positive work environment for both himself and his subordinates. A workplace with a conducive atmosphere can encourage the workers to remain in the socialization state, while also reducing their susceptibility to negative influences, such as stress and anxiety. In brief, drama, stress, and trauma are detrimental to organizational productivity, so leaders need to adopt innovative methods to eliminate them. We'll discuss this more later in the book.

Figure 3.4 illustrates the Polyvagal Ladder, highlighting through relatable body-language illustrations the importance of a positive work environment on everyone's well-being.

Figure 3.4 The Polyvagal Ladder

Source: Issue 50 Quick Bytes: Trauma Network for Children Part 3: Polyvagal Theory, https://www.healthxchange.sg/childtraumanetwork/Documents/Quick%20Bytes/Quick%20Bytes%20Issue%2050%20-%20Polyvagal%20Theory%20Part%203.pdf.

As you are aware, adverse factors contribute to a person's shift down the Polyvagal Ladder. As the stress level increases, the likelihood of the worker transitioning from the socialization state to the mobilization and immobilization states increases. For example, Maurer affirms that many recruiters were exposed to significant levels of stress during the global pandemic. Many organizations experienced staffing issues due to the loss of critical workers and the increased need to replace lost workers.[33] In addition, the global transition toward videoconferencing and online communication channels amplified the amount of stress recruiters faced during the pandemic.[34] These staffing burdens were transferred to recruiters, thereby influencing their decisions during talent acquisition. With takeaway lessons from the pandemic, we are even more aware of the need to create a conducive work environment in which workers can make optimal decisions. An environment with less drama and stress can encourage workers to shift from the other states back to the socialization state.

When the stressors that induce the transition down the Polyvagal Ladder are attributable to organizational factors, leaders must acknowledge that certain actions, practices, and policies are detrimental to the mental and emotional well-being of their employees. Human resource interventions that improve the organizational climate can improve the staff's well-being and performance.[35] So, if workplace drama, stress, and trauma are the leading causes of mobilization and immobilization in the organization, it is incumbent upon leaders to work toward eliminating internal and external triggers from the workplace.

Provide Safety Cues

A feeling of safety is essential to improving organizational staffing and productivity. Oliver's fight-or-flight behavior put the candidates and his staff on edge. While he tried to appear relaxed and friendly, research shows that an individual cannot be in both the socialization and mobilization or immobilization states simultaneously. Oliver really needed to take a breather and gain a fresh perspective on his challenges.

When the social engagement system is activated, the human body returns to its homeostatic state, which supports health, growth, and restoration.[36] This is a state from which employees have the opportunity to perform at their best and from which candidates can be more at ease during the interview process. Cues of safety, which include positive gestures, facial expressions, and encouraging vocalizations, can mitigate conditions that elicit defense and help someone who is not relaxed return to the socialization state.[37]

Research shows that cues of safety are an effective remedy for organizational stress and trauma. That said, in scenarios where trauma exposure is a predictable risk, leaders need to provide adequate psychological support to improve employees' well-being. Failure to promptly address employee trauma may leave the employer in a difficult position where they need to dedicate time and resources to address their workers' well-being without adversely affecting organizational productivity.[38] Overall, the main objective of safety cues is to increase the worker's or candidate's "window of tolerance" (see sidebar) and mitigate stress and trauma. (There's more on safety cues in Chapter 7.)

The Window of Tolerance

Just as different people have different autonomic baselines states, they also have varying levels of tolerance when faced with stressful or challenging situations and triggers. Some people naturally have a wider window of tolerance and are therefore able to adapt and respond more quickly than others. In *Clinical Applications of the Polyvagal Theory*, Stephen Porges and Deb Dana explain that this window of tolerance reflects the duration through which individuals trigger their social engagement system and restrict their autonomic system from reacting defensively.[39] Providing cues of safety in the workplace can keep the window open longer so that employees are not as likely to shift down the ladder in the face of challenging circumstances. Providing cues of safety during the selection process can mitigate the stress candidates may naturally feel when interviewing for a desired position.

Because everyone has their own window of tolerance, which can be wider or narrower depending on their personal and professional circumstances that particular day, a personal awareness of their own tolerance level in any given situation can provide people with important insight to recalibrate in order to keep the window from shutting entirely. By using safety cues, an instinctive leader can insert a wedge in the window frame—their own as well as others'.

KEY POINTS

- Bias and discrimination can manifest in several ways during the interview and selection process and become more pronounced if the recruiter has descended the Polyvagal Ladder as a result of stress.
- Aside from taking the usual considerations into account, candidates should be assessed for their baseline autonomic state to help determine if they are a good fit for the position.
- Creating accurate job descriptions that reflect the characteristics of the job environment in addition to the responsibilities of the role provides a clear benchmark for evaluating applicants.
- Identifying applicant groups that are highly vulnerable to bias will reduce the subconscious influences to discount those groups.
- Providing safety cues helps workers and potential recruits remain in or return to the socialization rung on the Polyvagal Ladder.

CHAPTER 4

Achieving Financial Success Using Your Sixth Sense

Numerous challenges and opportunities arise in humanity's pursuit of financial success. Rational thought drives us to make decisions regarding our investments and expenditures based on analysis. In contrast, nonrational thought, which relies on instinct and intuition, can result in a range of outcomes—from errors to breakthroughs. In this chapter, we'll look at how these two cognitive processes influence financial decision-making with an emphasis on embracing both the rational and nonrational components of our mental faculties to attain success in the financial sector. We'll also look at how bias arises in this sector when making decisions as well as at the impacts of stress and trauma on financial decision-making. Our main objective in this chapter is to clarify how to navigate autonomic states in intense and high-pressured finance-related situations. Oliver Green's case will highlight how the components of the Polyvagal Theory shape the subconscious thoughts of business leaders in the financial sector.

Oliver Green has delivered outstanding performance as a financial trader in the last few years. His main role has been to purchase and sell shares and equities for various clients. He has become quite proficient at projecting the future value of financial assets. His promotion to senior executive reflects that he has become an expert not only in financial trading but presumably also in leadership and human resource management. He understands that money is a valuable tool used by most organizations to drive their workers to deliver their full potential. However, there are many scenarios where Oliver is conflicted by this ideology. In some situations, his decisions are based on cold and calculated analysis. Some inevitably end in failure or severe losses. As a financial trader, Oliver understands that poor decisions can have detrimental impacts on the trader as well as the entire organization.

From Oliver's perspective, his main problem is his insufficient understanding of organizational decision-making. Despite his high academic and professional qualifications, Oliver acknowledges that he lacks the mental awareness to distinguish between instinctive and logical decisions. As a young senior executive, there are many situations where he needs to restrain his decisions so that he does not succumb to bias, moods, or personal emotions. He has been struggling to balance his personal and professional responsibilities to the extent that it has begun harming his financial decisions. In some situations, Oliver follows popular market trends when he makes stock decisions, but in others, he avoids making decisions because he fears his investors will experience disastrous losses. Oliver has made several financial errors, so he often avoids making any decisions that seem too risky. Unwillingness to take risks is disadvantageous in the financial sector, especially when decisions need to be made without adequate time or resources. Oliver is not certain whether he has the sixth sense for financial decision-making. He needs to develop a mindset that will safeguard him from bias or discrimination in his pursuit of financial success. Is instinctive decision-making possible for young leaders like Oliver?

Financial Decision-Making in the Twenty-First Century

Many researchers have attributed humanity's pursuit of excellence to globalization and capitalism, while others have claimed that societal growth is determined by the society's pursuit of intrinsic needs. For instance, globalization has encouraged many workers to pursue financial benefits and professional excellence. Research shows that although financial globalization seems like a concept that emerged in the 1970s, its roots can be traced to the early 1900s when society started embracing capitalist and market-oriented structures.[1] Whether we are talking about financial success or societal growth, both rational and nonrational thinking play vital roles. The rational component encourages people to pursue safe and realistic rewards, whereas the nonrational component drives them to take risks that can help them achieve their goals. As society continues to experience challenges and changes, leaders need to understand how to balance their rational and nonrational faculties to leverage their full cognitive capabilities to achieve financial success.

Although many people place a lot of value on intangible rewards, such as professional recognition and job satisfaction, the reality is that tangible rewards have become vital drivers of human behaviors in the twenty-first century. Nevertheless, it is common for employees to leave their jobs due to negative perceptions of their work environment. On one hand, a positive work environment distributes rewards in accordance with the employees' contributions, thereby improving the productivity of the workers and the entire organization. On the other hand, a negative work environment discourages workers from delivering their full potential. For instance, employee punishments such as oral reprimands tend to have adverse effects on staff morale and productivity. This rationale explains why many organizations seek to create warm and positive work atmospheres for their employees that drive them to deliver optimal productivity. Overall, financial decision-making in the twenty-first century requires leaders to maneuver through various internal and external factors to strengthen the staff's productivity.

The Mechanisms Behind Financial Decision-Making

Numerous concepts have emerged that attempt to describe the rational and nonrational dimensions of decision-making in the financial sector. Considering the rapid evolution of business and financial systems in the modern market, leaders are facing new challenges in their respective positions. Although most leaders undergo extensive training to develop their current knowledge and skills, these competencies are inadequate for cultivating instinctive decision-making. The basic financial market can be summarized using a buy-sell ideology. This ideology encourages business stakeholders to make decisions prioritizing the risk and reward tradeoffs of the transaction. Most leaders pursue investments that offer the greatest rewards and the least risk. Nonetheless, predicting optimal business decisions is quite challenging in the real-life market due to variable microeconomic and macroeconomic factors. This problem can worsen in situations when the professional is affected by adverse influences, such as stress and trauma, which could encourage them to make decisions that exceed an individual's or business's financial tolerance.

In the real world, many external variables can influence a person's disposition toward certain investment decisions and their overall financial tolerance. Some researchers claim that a person's age can determine their financial goals and objectives. For example, Frydman and Camerer claim that people who grew up during the Great Depression are more likely to avoid transactions that result in corporate debt.[2] The younger generations, in contrast, are less risk-averse. The Great Depression aside, age can be a determining factor specifically due to less or more time for investments to mature as well as lived experience. These researchers also determined that the gender of a leader can influence their choices: many female managers at the senior level were found to be less aggressive than their male counterparts with regard to financial resources and tax savings.[3] Although these findings do not represent all market situations, they do indicate that the financial market has factors that induce implicit and explicit bias. Let's begin to identify these causes by comparing objective and subjective trading.

Objective Versus Subjective Trading

Objective and subjective trading are popular ideologies that reflect the popular decision-making styles in the modern finance sector. Whereas objective trading relies on established rules and analysis, subjective trading incorporates an intuitive understanding of the market and human behavior. Oliver Green's example will help clarify this.

As a young trader, Oliver has dedicated a lot of time and effort to understanding the rules of stock trading. The basics are relatively simple: buy when an asset's price drops below the moving average and sell when the asset moves above that level. These principles are relatively simple to Oliver who has comprehensive training and education regarding the financial market. However, this objective approach often prevents him from seeing the full picture of the financial market. As time progresses, Oliver understands that there is more to the market than simply buying or selling assets. At this point, Oliver begins reviewing the factors that can cause spikes or slumps in a corporation's assets. This approach enlightens Oliver that the market is quite complicated. Many external factors can influence the prices of the market, and these variables cannot be evaluated from an objective viewpoint. Perhaps, the subjective style will allow Oliver to understand the overall financial market. In brief, he needs to ascertain whether the objective or subjective style will allow him to achieve his professional ambitions.

A major ideology in financial trading involves the distinction between objective and subjective trading. These two categories reflect the traders' decisions to follow the market rules or their personal perceptions when making stock decisions. Foremost, objective traders often prefer to follow a specific set of rules and guidelines when making financial decisions. These professionals have a preference for preestablished rules, and their responses to the market are based on the judgments toward specific trading opportunities. Objective trading is considered the simplest way to trade because it relies on a defined set of rules; hence, it is designed for automatic responses to the market.[4] In such a market, the trader has the opportunity to monitor trades and abandon investments that result in losses. This trading style is considered the conventional approach to financial trading, especially for new traders who lack adequate skill and experience. Evidently, the objective approach is less susceptible to bias than the objective approach.

In comparison, subjective traders are often easily swayed by their emotions and behavioral components when making trading decisions. For that reason, subjective trading is aligned with instinctive thinking, whereas objective trading is associated with analytical decision-making. With that said, subjective trading is more appropriate for experienced traders who are conversant with market patterns.[5] These professionals have a comprehensive understanding of financial market dynamics to the extent of developing an instinctive comprehension of market patterns. Although these traders are more susceptible to bias and discrimination, their choices are usually more reflective of the financial market than the choices objective traders are. The distinction between objective and subjective trading is illustrated in Figure 4.1.

Figure 4.1 Objective Versus Subjective Trading

Source: Park, M. (2023, February 24). Objective vs. Subjective Trading, Corporate Finance Institute. https://corporatefinanceinstitute.com/resources/capital-markets/objective-vs-subjective-trading/

As you can see from Figure 4.1, objective trading and subjective trading are vastly different constructs. Objective trading, which relies on rational thinking, seems quite rigid is in its application, whereas subjective trading, which incorporates the "sixth sense," allows ample room for traders to exercise their intuition and experience. There's obviously a place for both approaches, but overall, a disciplined long-term approach tends to be most successful. The subjective approach, when exercised from the sympathetic state, is associated with gambling and unnecessary risk-taking, so there's more potential for poor choices and loss. That said, investors who can remain calm in the parasympathetic state are more likely to rely on objective trading elements while still accessing subjective trading elements—in other words, they use both rational and nonrational thought processes.

Developing the Sixth Sense in Financial Decision-Making

The Polyvagal Theory encourages the belief that human actions can be predicted based on the surrounding environment. Accordingly, the perceptions of the surrounding environment provide clues to financial decision makers that allow them to evaluate the risks and rewards of certain choices. In this context, this ability is labeled the sixth sense in accordance with the objectives of instinctive leadership. For traders, instinct and gut feelings are important indicators of the potential of an investment, provided they are accessing this from a parasympathetic (ventral vagal) state.

Research conducted by the University of Cambridge and the Queensland University of Technology reveal that gut feelings are derived from the human perceptions of their surroundings.[6] *Interoception* describes a person's ability to sense their physiological processes, such as the pace of their heartbeat and other internal sensations. Interoception is the reason we experience "gut feelings." The researchers set forth that gut feelings are sensations that convey information between the brain and essential tissues, such as the heart, lungs, and gut. They sought to investigate whether interoception and gut feelings can offer insights into a person's financial decisions and recruited 18 traders from recognized hedge funds who handle the purchase and sale of various business assets.

The primary objective of the investigation was to analyze whether stock traders can make accurate instinctive responses from market information. In addition, this investigation was performed during the particularly challenging time of Europe's sovereign debt crisis (aka the Eurozone Crisis). As a result, the findings of the investigation reflect the behaviors of financial traders in both safe and critical market situations. In the end, the investigation revealed that traders rely on subconscious and physiological signs to understand trading signs. This investigation highlights the importance of relying on the sixth sense, or nonrational thought processes, when making financial decisions.[7]

One of the researchers who participated in the investigation claimed, "We're looking instead at risk-takers' physiology—how good are they at sensing signals from their viscera? We should refocus on the body, or more exactly the interaction between body and brain. Medics find this obvious; economists don't."[8] This statement suggests that financial trading decisions can be evaluated by assessing the autonomic nervous responses between the body and the brain. These findings underscore the value of exercising the sixth sense along with the other five senses to strengthen neuroception and interoception for the purpose of making well-rounded decisions.

The Ups and Downs of Financial Decision-Making

As a result of his accurate financial projections, Oliver often experiences a lot of pressure from his supervisors and subordinates to make profitable financial decisions. This pressure has been gradually increasing since his promotion to senior executive to the extent that it is now adversely affecting his financial investment decisions. Oliver is usually ecstatic when he identifies a suitable business opportunity. He has a tendency to increase his investments when he feels that a particular share or equity will offer significant returns. At this point, his euphoria encourages him to invest in more shares and equities. Nonetheless, he also evaluates his choices to ascertain whether there is a possibility of encountering failure or unexpected losses. When the stock market returns are unsuccessful, Oliver begins to fear that his decision-making process was faulty. He hopes that his skills as a long-term investor will allow him to recoup his losses, but all signs indicate that he has lost his investment know-how.

As the stock market returns continue to worsen, Oliver begins to consider whether he should surrender. Another risky gamble is to continue to buy shares while everyone is cautious. Perhaps this gamble will allow him to recoup his losses. With that said, Oliver has returned to the state of optimism where he believes his decisions will result in maximum returns. Oliver needs to remove himself from this cycle of poor financial decisions.

Oliver's scenario illusrates what we all know: the financial sector is characterized by numerous internal and external challenges. The main ideology in this market is that financial success leads to positive psychological states, whereas financial failure tends to lead to negative psychological states, thereby causing the fight, flight, or freeze response. This phenomenon is illustrated in Figure 4.2.

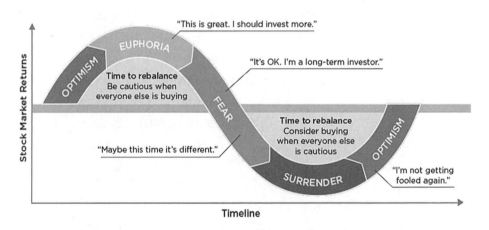

Figure 4.2 Investor's Behaviors in Different Market Cycles

Source: VanderPal, G., & Brazie, R. (2022). Influence of Basic Human Behaviors (Influenced by Brain Architecture and Function), and Past Traumatic Events on Investor Behavior and Financial Bias, *Journal of Accounting and Finance 22*(2).

The figure illustrates how financial trading often follows a specific cycle. In this cycle, the stock trader is likely to undergo the following emotions: optimism, euphoria, fear, and surrender. In other circumstances, the financial trader may move from surrender to optimism, depending on their inherent desire for the transaction. These emotional stages can sway a financial trader's decisions, potentially leading to poor investments. These transitions may compel the trader to make false assumptions due to erroneous beliefs. Let's take a look at each of these emotional stages and the thought processes behind them in Table 4.1.

Table 4.1 Investor Behaviors in the Financial Trading Cycle

Emotional Stage	Thought Process	Example
Optimism	*I want this stock. It feels like a good investment.*	Oliver identifies a feasible market opportunity that can offer significant financial returns. This is the socialization state.
Euphoria	*This is great! I should invest more capital in this opportunity.*	Oliver feels that this opportunity is too good to pass up. He invests more capital in the opportunity. His euphoria indicates a dip into the mobilization state.
Fear	*It's OK. I'm a long-term investor.* *Maybe it's different this time.*	Based on the low returns, Oliver starts to fear that he's made the wrong investment decision. His only option is to console himself. This stage marks a full transition to the mobilization state.
Surrender	*Maybe I should avoid these types of investments.* *Maybe I should take more risks.*	Oliver feels hopeless. He transitions to the immobilization state due to his growing fear of loss due to poor investments.
Optimism	*I won't be fooled again.*	Fear makes Oliver a more cautious financial trader. He believes he will not succumb to poor financial investments in the future. This suggests a shift back to mobilization and then potentially socialization.

As you can see from Table 4.1, to escape this typical market cycle, Oliver Green needs to understand how these investment mindsets are the result of the state of his autonomic nervous system. Decisions made in any state other than from the socialization state are seldom reliable. In the mobilization state (which includes euphoria) as well as in the immobilization state, one's gut instinct, or sixth sense, can be clouded by irrational thought processes rather than being driven by rational and nonrational thinking. Oliver needs to learn to climb back up the ladder to a position where he can trust his decisions.

The Emergence of Bias in Financial Decision-Making

The human mind (both conscious and subconscious) is an intricate tapestry that's woven by an individual's beliefs of the world. At any given moment, a person's beliefs can determine their expectations of experiences as well as their future actions. This rationale explains why most researchers support the belief that the human mind was designed to support predictive coding based on the surrounding environment.[9] So, if the brain detects an error that deviates from the mind's prediction, it triggers a response aimed at correcting the error. This error-correcting response can trigger the sympathetic nervous system and the dorsal vagal complex, thereby inducing mobilization or immobilization, respectively. Although this process seems relatively complicated, it can be simplified by clarifying the mechanisms through which the human brain evaluates financial decision-making. These deductions are essential for revealing how leaders can take *full* advantage of their cognitive faculties.

Types of Bias in Financial Decision-Making

Workers in the financial sector need to safeguard themselves from several types of biases, including over-confidence bias, self-serving bias, herd mentality, loss aversion, framing cognitive bias, anchoring bias, con-firmation bias, representativeness heuristic bias, and recency bias. These biases are aligned with the con-scious and subconscious elements of the human brain. Although many people struggle to make fair, unbiased decisions, the reality is that there are many situations in which their choices are influenced by implicit or explicit variables. Additionally, being a state of sympathetic activation (mobilization) or dorsal vagal collapse (immo-bilization) can impact this process. Table 4.2 provides a brief overview of these biases along with thoughts and actions a trader may have in response to the bias. Again, we'll use Oliver as an example, but to be clear, each sce-nario stands alone. Thereafter, we'll take a more in-depth look at each type of bias.

Table 4.2 Types of Bias in Financial Decision-Making

Bias Type	Description	Financial Sector Example
Overconfidence bias	Occurs when a leader has false (exaggerated) beliefs about their compe-tency or skills.	Oliver believes that every deci-sion he makes will lead to profits and every lost investment will be recovered regardless of how impossible it seems.
Self-serving bias	Emerges when a leader believes they can accurately pre-dict market trends.	Oliver believes that he is the best stock trader in the com-pany. Sometimes he makes lucky guesses, but he attributes these guesses to his clever thinking.

(continued)

Table 4.2 Types of Bias in Financial Decision-Making *(continued)*

Bias Type	Description	Financial Sector Example
Herd mentality bias	Manifests when a business leader follows popular market trends instead of their personal or professional analysis.	Oliver claims that the market is never wrong. For that reason, he is the first to invest in popular stocks, as well as the first to abandon stocks with negative publicity.
Loss aversion bias	Emerges when a leader fears losses more than they desire to make profits. As a result, the leader stagnates in uncertainty.	Oliver has made many bad financial decisions, so he often rejects investments that may incur losses. Oliver does not understand that every business can incur profit or loss.
Framing cognitive bias	Occurs based on the positive framing of information to encourage certain groups to pursue a specific action.	Oliver understands that some business investments are too risky. However, he portrays the investments as profitable regardless of whether the investors experience profit or loss.
Anchoring bias	Manifests when a leader places too much emphasis on preconceived information to the extent of neglecting current information.	Oliver believes that buying shares or equities from a certain company will always lead to profits. This belief is ingrained regardless of whether the company experiences profit or loss.
Confirmation bias	Occurs when a leader makes decisions to confirm that their beliefs are true.	Oliver always encourages customers to buy stock from a certain company. He wants to prove these stocks are the most profitable ones in the market.
Representativeness heuristic bias	Emerges when a leader makes false assumptions about the relationships of different items or events.	Oliver believes that some financial stock events are related. For that reason, he believes he can identify similar relationships in other stock events.
Recency bias	Occurs when a leader believes that recent events in the financial sector will reoccur. As a result, the leader may neglect alternatives.	Oliver recently experienced a situation where a rise in a company's stocks caused a corresponding rise in a rival's stocks. Due to this event, Oliver believes that the market will soon show a similar response.

Overconfidence bias. This type of bias often emerges due to a person's false perception of their skill, talent, or personal belief.[10] Accordingly, this bias is quite hazardous in the financial sector.[11] Overconfidence bias often manifests in different ways. For instance, a stock trader may develop illusions of control that sway them to make decisions that do not reflect the market. In other situations, the worker may make hypotheses that are aligned with their personal projections of the financial market. Furthermore, these assumptions may worsen in stressful or traumatic scenarios where the person embraces these false beliefs because they lack a rational perspective.[12] Leaders need to safeguard themselves from succumbing to overconfidence bias to avoid negatively impacting their financial outcomes.

Self-serving bias. This type of bias is relatively common in the financial sector. Many workers in this sector make decisions based on the belief that these choices will lead them to personal financial success. Self-serving bias stems from a person's tendency to attribute outcomes to their skills or competencies.[13] For instance, a leader may attribute financial success to their good decision-making when their success is actually dependent on luck and chance encounters. Therefore, self-serving bias can prevent stock traders from recognizing the contributions of other parties due to their pursuit of personal benefits.

Herd mentality bias. This type of bias occurs when a person prioritizes the opinions of the majority over their own personal assessments. In the stock trading business, this type of mentality is quite common because people have a tendency to pursue marketing opportunities where other people have recorded success. As a result, this mentality can encourage leaders to make emotional or irrational choices due to their perceptions of their surrounding environment. By following popular market trends, some leaders believe they can minimize losses and increase their accumulated profits.

Loss aversion bias. This type of bias is the opposite of overconfidence bias. Loss aversion bias often occurs when the investor fears making decisions that may result in losses. In such situations, the investor's fear may overwhelm their pursuit of success to the extent of avoiding decisions that may offer more profits than losses. The instinctive fear of losses may drive a person to avoid harmful or stressful events, thereby preventing them from accurately identifying profitable ventures. The expected risks and returns of financial decisions cannot be fully ascertained, so leaders need to develop mechanisms for evaluating whether the pros outweigh the cons.

Framing cognitive bias. Although this type of bias is not common in the organizational environment, it is quite prevalent in the financial sector. Framing bias occurs when a leader presents information in a way that manipulates the audience, instead of providing the actual accounts of the event. For instance, a leader may proclaim that stock from a certain company will increase in value, when the reality is that the stock will increase in value by a diminutive amount. Many stock traders make decisions based on how information is framed rather than on the actual accounts.

Anchoring bias. This bias emerges when a leader uses preexisting information as a reference for subsequent conclusions. These types of assumptions can skew decision-making in favor of preconceived notions. For instance, a leader may become dependent on historical information without understanding that the data can change depending on the current circumstances. Furthermore, the situation can worsen in situations where the leader's decisions are affected by stress or trauma.[14] In the financial market, up-to-date information can make a significant difference in terms of distinguishing between profitable and wasteful investments.

Confirmation bias. This bias is similar to anchoring bias, but it encourages leaders to pursue decisions that confirm their hypotheses. Confirmation bias is based on the notion that leaders often make choices that align with their expectations and beliefs. As a result, these notions can prevent them from making fair choices. Accordingly, many leaders make safe and comfortable decisions due to the belief that their choices will lead to positive outcomes. Confirmation bias can prevent leaders from discerning the true reality of their organizational situations.

Representativeness heuristic bias. This bias occurs when a leader believes in perceived correlations between different items. For instance, a stock trader may develop the assumption that stock from two companies with similar characteristics will develop the same response. This approach often encourages leaders to make decisions, believing that their choices will result in similar outcomes as previous situations. However, the reality is that human beings lack the ability to accurately determine whether two items have an intrinsic relationship. Wise investors need to understand how to evaluate events and items as individual components to make accurate decisions.

Recency bias. This type of bias manifests when a leader believes that recent events will transpire again soon. The relationships between most events can be predicted based on previous interactions. As a result, recency bias occurs when a person develops a preference for recent events instead of historical ones. Recency bias can occur when a leader believes that previous market events symbolize that the company will experience a particular change. This change can be positive or negative, depending on the leader's projections. Leaders need to safeguard themselves from succumbing to recency bias to make effective decisions that safeguard the corporation's short-term and long-term vision.

The Impact of Stress and Trauma on Financial Decision-Making

From Oliver Green's perspective, financial decision-making is his passion. To his dismay, he has been experiencing challenges when making financial decisions for the company's clients and other business investors. As a result of his promotion to senior executive, he is overloaded with work and some responsibilities that take him outside his comfort zone. When the workday is over, Oliver is left with little to no energy to enjoy his downtime. He figured this was par for the course; the promotion would obviously require more effort and energy from him, so he treated the matter as trivial and simply tried to get to bed earlier—that is, until the day he made a huge mistake during a particular financial assessment. The organization lost a major client due to his mistake, and now, whenever he makes financial decisions, this event is at the back of his mind. This trauma has started to affect Oliver's behavior at work and at home. Some days, he feels like he should just stay home because he doesn't feel up to facing more stress and the other adverse emotions. He predicts his days as a senior executive will always be filled with stress and frustration. Clearly, Oliver requires an innovative method for eliminating stress in his workplace and mitigating the potential for trauma.

As you can see, Oliver is suffering from overwhelming stress as well as a traumatic experience (losing a client as a result of his mistake) that has caused him to question his abilities. His increased workload and responsibilities are major concerns that contribute to his daily exhaustion. These issues mobilized Oliver's physiological resources to shift him from the socialization to the mobilization state. In extreme situations, Oliver shows that he fears making major decisions because he dreads losing other customers due to even minor mistakes. This change reflects his transition to the immobilization state, where decision-making is skewed in favor of the "freeze" state. With proper education and training, Oliver can learn skills to regulate his nervous system to help address negative psychological issues and regain his confidence as a financial trader, which will improve the organization's overall performance.

Stress and trauma are, unfortunately, common variables in the modern organizational environment and specifically in the financial sector where financial stability is on the line. Moreover, the challenge of resolving financial disputes can be enormously stressful. Research shows that some financial workers experience more stress than others due to their unique responsibilities. For instance, debt collectors tend to face more challenges than regular financial workers.[15] This is because debtors can be combative and defensive, especially if they are lacking funds. Furthermore, stress often poses adverse effects on employee morale and satisfaction, so it can easily encourage employees to leave the organization prematurely. Specifically with regard to financial decision-making, stress can skew financial choices in alignment with the following factors: a person's inability to manage debt, overspending tendencies, low income, and insufficient knowledge regarding effective spending habits.[16]

In the workplace, employees who are stressed to their limits may exhibit the following signs: absenteeism, frequent requests for time off, wage garnishments, and advance pay requests.[17] These signs point to low satisfaction in the work environment due to any number of reasons.

Risk Tolerance

Financial investment is strongly dependent on a leader's ability to be willing to take risks, as few investments come with a 100 percent satisfaction guarantee. However, different people have varying risk-tolerance levels, which is an important consideration. While some individuals are most comfortable with the "safest" decisions, others are more attuned toward risky financial investments. A range of factors come into play regarding one's risk tolerance. For example, research by Fuochi and Conzo explains that a person's exposure to trauma can influence financial risk tolerance.[18] According to scholars, exposure to trauma can reduce a person's tolerance levels, thereby encouraging them to either avoid or overly engage in risky investments. In comparison, low exposure to trauma can increase a person's awareness of risks and rewards.

In general, people who are operating from the sympathetic state tend to be averse to taking risks, and those operating from the dorsal vagal parasympathetic state tend to avoid any risk. Since some risk is obviously necessary when it comes to financial investments, leaders need to rely on their rational and nonrational thought processes to weigh and evaluate the pros and cons and decide what level of risk is acceptable in any given opportunity. This can best be achieved from a state of balance.

Applying the Polyvagal Theory to Improve Financial Decision-Making

Few studies have been conducted on the relationship between the Polyvagal Theory and financial decision-making. However, several links exist between financial decision-making and rational and nonrational thinking, which correspond to the theory. The principle of rational decision-making in the finance sector stems from economic considerations and investment theories. For instance, neoclassical theories such as self-interest and return maximization are considered strong drivers of rational decision-making. However, despite these considerations, the real-life market is characterized by both predictable and unpredictable market events. Predictable events can be resolved using conventional rational approaches, whereas unpredictable events may compel the leader to integrate nonrational strategies, such as instinct. Furthermore, leaders need to take into account the impacts of stress and trauma on risk-taking and risk-aversive behaviors. Therefore, the Polyvagal Theory is a crucial framework for identifying the best responses for augmenting financial success. Further research is clearly warranted. In the meantime, nurturing instinctive financial decision-making can be achieved by doing the following two things.

Balance Rational and Nonrational Decision-Making

We have been stressing the need to balance rational and nonrational decision-making throughout this book. In our fictitious example, Oliver needs to understand when to apply rational decision-making and/or nonrational decision-making (his "sixth sense") to improve his outcomes—that is, whether to take an objective or subjective approach, or a combination of the two. While many researchers claim that emotions are an impediment to optimal decision-making, neuroeconomics research proves that emotional decision-making is linked to the neural components that evaluate risks and rewards,[19] which is an essential part of good investment strategies. Incidentally, simple actions like interacting with a person of the opposite gender can cause subconscious flaws in a person's investment choices.[20] Situations such as these support the perception that emotional stimuli are *detrimental* influences on decision-making. However, interoception (the body's internal signals) and neuroception (the process that determines a specific physiological response to the environment) trigger our emotional responses to stimuli. These responses can provide important information, provided that no danger is perceived to send the person into a sympathetic state. When accessed from the socialization state, "gut instincts" driven by emotion can offer valuable insights when considering an investment opportunity.

Considering that no one is immune to emotional stimuli, in general, instinctive leaders need to acknowledge the benefits of incorporating nonrational factors into the management structure and decision-making process. By striving for an equilibrium between rational and nonrational decision-making, financial traders can merge the benefits of both mental faculties for the best possible outcomes.

Support Somatic Experiencing in the Workplace

Somatic Experiencing is a body-oriented therapeutic approach in which the person, or in this case the worker, tunes in to their bodily sensations rather than their thoughts and emotions, as one would in cognitive therapy. It helps the person recognize the state of their autonomic nervous system, thereby cultivating an awareness of interoception, allowing this "skill" to be strengthened, while releasing stored tension and trauma in the nervous system that can keep one stuck in a fight, flight, or freeze response. This therapeutic approach can be applied by multiple professionals in different work settings to heal trauma, chronic stress, and other conditions.[21]

It would behoove Oliver, who has been in a loop of chronic stress, to enroll in and encourage his subordinates to join therapy groups that promote somatic experiences. The key objective of Somatic Experiencing is to recover and strengthen a person's decision-making faculties to improve their overall well-being. Somatic Experiencing combines the findings of multidisciplinary research regarding physiology, psychology, neuroscience, biology, medical biophysics, and ethology.[22] The main goal of Somatic Experiencing is to give employees the opportunity to discharge negative emotions that drive a person to shift across the states of the Polyvagal Ladder—from socialization to mobilization to immobilization—and bring them back to the socialization/safety state.

KEY POINTS

- Emotional, or nonrational, decision-making, which we have referred to as the sixth sense or gut instinct, is linked to the neural components that evaluate risks and rewards, making this thought process just as valuable as rational thought when making financial decisions.

- Leaders need to use both their rational and nonrational faculties to leverage their full cognitive capabilities to optimize their decisions. In the financial sector, this requires a balance between subjective and objective approaches to investments.

- Human behaviors are driven by the environment coupled with past experiences, affecting how a person evaluates financial risks and rewards. Having experienced financial trauma will usually result in lower risk tolerance, driving home the need to weigh the pros and cons from an objective perspective.

- Several biases tend to influence financial decision-making, especially while in the sympathetic state. Awareness of these biases helps to mitigate a leader's sway on decision-making, as does taking steps to return the body to the parasympathetic state.

- Somatic Experiencing therapy is an approach that helps the body recover from stress and trauma. It is one of many established interventions that may help to reduce the effects of stress and trauma on the autonomic nervous system. The benefits of this approach include more freedom, satisfaction, enjoyment, and, of course, clearheaded decision-making in the financial sector and beyond.

CHAPTER 5

Creating Superior Teams

So far, we've looked at how the Polyvagal Theory relates to the organizational setting, how it affects leadership, its impacts on organizational staffing and talent acquisition, and its effects on financial decision-making. We've made a solid case for finding the sweet spot between relying on rational and nonrational thinking, and how simply being aware of our biases and physical state can result in positive changes. In this chapter, we'll turn our attention to how organizational leaders can use the three autonomic states to improve staff productivity. We'll start with a scenario where senior executive Oliver Green creates conflict during a department meeting, and later we'll see how he can solve the team conflict with an approach based on the Polyvagal Theory. We'll also narrow down the characteristics that define good team leaders and followers and explore the mechanisms for improving conflict resolution in the workplace. We'll conclude this chapter with a discussion of how leaders can provide safety cues to improve employees' well-being and organizational productivity.

Ever since his promotion to senior executive, Oliver has dedicated a lot of effort to improving the performance of the workers in his department. However, his department has been illustrating inconsistent performance throughout his tenure as the senior executive. Although Oliver tried different strategies to improve the department's outcomes, he was unable to achieve consistent results. After the department received the lowest performance in its history, Oliver was compelled to call a department meeting to discuss the issue and identify feasible solutions for addressing the problem.

Oliver acknowledges that he needs his subordinates' input to implement appropriate recommendations. He begins by calling out workers who demonstrated the highest and lowest results during the period. Afterward, Oliver starts evaluating the reasons each employee attained their respective performances. While the hardworking performers seem grateful for the recognition, the low performers feel they are being attacked. As a result, the meeting escalates into a major argument between Oliver and his subordinates, as well as between the team members themselves.

Furthermore, some members were unable to respond to Oliver's accusations. Oliver fears that his approach may have worsened the situation and the relationships between the department's staff.

How might Oliver rectify the situation and positively improve the synergy between himself as the team leader and his subordinates?

Causes of Team Conflicts

Team conflicts can emerge for multiple reasons. These reasons may be major organizational issues or trivial personal issues. Nonetheless, it is vital to realize that the team leader's and members' autonomic states are vital for guiding the outcomes of team conflicts. Good teams are composed of members who can be guided from the mobilization and immobilization states back to the socialization state (which we'll discuss more as we go). This phenomenon is illustrated in Figure 5.1.

Notice how the curve begins at social engagement where the situation is grounded and settled, and workers see themselves as being on the same team. Everything is satisfactory to all. In the face of circumstances that arouse the sympathetic system (like Oliver's botched department meeting), they become swept up in unproductive, defensive emotional reactions, possibly working their way up to complete shutdown. It's up to the leader to help the workers return to social engagement where they once again perceive a safe environment.

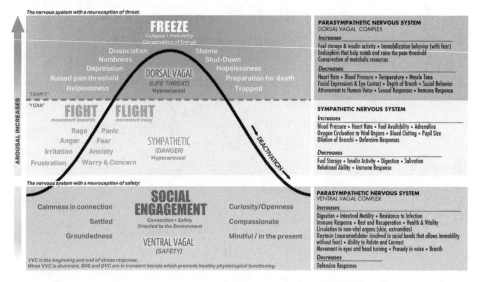

Figure 5.1 Deactivation of the Defensive States

Source: A, A. (2019, September 22). Arriving in Presence: Overcoming Depersonalization—Derealization Disorder. Medium. https://medium.com/ @andreyvukolov_53472/arriving-in-presence-overcoming-depersonalization -derealization-disorder-516b46be81c1

Characteristics of Good Teams

In Oliver's case, a good team would support his decisions and allow him to improve the department's productivity. Good teamwork requires the leader and the team members to be unified to drive the department to achieve its goals. The workers need to demonstrate through attitude, behavior, and action that they are committed to improving the department's productivity. However, Oliver's case illustrates that teamwork is impractical or unrealistic in some situations, indicating that changes are required. For instance, team members may be quick to begin conflicts or disputes with each other if they perceive they are being attacked. In other cases, the leader or the organization may be creating conditions that cause worker dissatisfaction. The leader and team need to analyze whether the working environment or the team interactions are the root causes of conflicts. The leader and team need to reflect on the drivers and barriers that influence communication within the department in an effort to strengthen relationships among team members.

A well-composed team should allow the members to provide complementary knowledge and skills to the collective. Bell and colleagues demonstrate teamwork using the ABC framework of teams, shown in Figure 5.2. According to the researchers, decision-making in teams is a component of three states: affective states, behavioral states, and cognitive states.[1] First, the affective states describe the team members' attitudes and feelings toward the collective and its tasks—for example, mood,

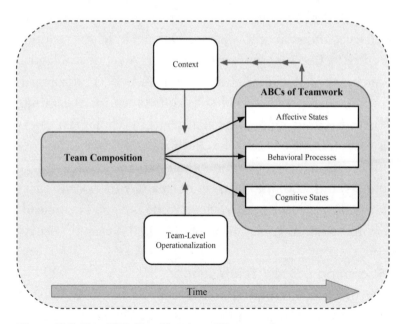

Figure 5.2 The ABC Classification of Teamwork

Source: Bell, S. T., Brown, S.G., Colaneri, A., & Outland, N. (2018). Team Composition and the ABCs of Teamwork, *American Psychologist 73*(4), 349.

trust, and cohesion. In comparison, the behavioral states describe the inputs and outputs (i.e., actions) dedicated by the team members to the collective—for example, collaborating with others. The cognitive state reflects the structure of knowledge exchange in the organization.[2] With enough time, the team leader and members can build strong relationships with each other that are mutually beneficial in a way that's as simple as ABC.

A well-composed team also requires a leader with the ability to reflect on their own subjectivity as well as that of the team members. This is an essential skill in team settings that allows the leader to identify critical issues. Reflection allows the leader to understand how their characteristics correlate with the behaviors of the collective. Research shows that reflective functioning and team cognition revolve around the organized cognitive structures that allow the leader and team members to share, retrieve, and store knowledge.[3] Deficits in team cognition and reflective functioning can lead to psychopathological outcomes (behavioral dysfunction and social disorganization) and poor psychological outcomes for the group. These findings emphasize that team psychological safety is essential for creating an equilibrium between the cognitive behaviors of the individual and the collective.[4] To understand the importance of team functioning, let's break down the characteristics that define good team leaders and team members by applying the Polyvagal Theory.

Becoming a Good Team Leader

The first step for improving the team dynamics in Oliver's department is to encourage Oliver to cultivate good team leadership skills. Oliver's tendency to use an authoritative leadership style is a major issue in the department that has contributed to many conflicts. Accordingly, Oliver needs to evaluate the characteristics that can strengthen his leadership skills. These traits include transcendence, drive, collaboration, humanity, humility, integrity, temperance, justice, accountability, courage, and good judgment. Among these traits, good judgment can allow Oliver to control his autonomic responses by taking into account all aspects of a situation, thereby preventing him from falling into the mobilization or immobilization state. In a nutshell, a leader needs to be able to discern when to stand firm on a decision (i.e., be dominant) and when to be open to differing perspectives and adjust according to the majority (i.e., be submissive).

Over the years, many changes have occurred regarding society's perceptions of team leaders and collective decision-making in the organizational context. Research shows that the last decade has seen scholars emphasizing a shift from vertical and hierarchical structures to horizontal and collective processes.[5] In this context, the focus is placed on collective leadership strategies and the effect of socialization and mobilization among team leaders. Team leaders are usually characterized by their high reliance on the socialization and mobilization systems to improve decision-making. The social engagement system is essential for guiding social interactions between the leader and subordinates, whereas the mobilization system is vital for encouraging the leader to determine whether they should confront or avoid a specific situation. In this case, the combination of the ventral vagal complex (the parasympathetic state) and sympathetic nervous system can strengthen the leader's social interactions and also improve their awareness of organizational issues. To be clear, however, we've been focusing much of our discussion on the fight-or-flight response with regard to the sympathetic state. As noted earlier, there's a distinction between being triggered to fight or flee and being in the "I can" state of mobilization, which is devoid of fear or anger and does not increase in intensity.

As we mentioned earlier, among the main characteristics of team leaders, the most important one is good judgment. Team leaders should have the ability to make good judgments regardless of the level of uncertainty or ambiguity surrounding the situation. Judgment is required in each stage of the leadership process, as illustrated in Figure 5.3. The second most prominent trait is courage.[6] Courage allows the leader to confront challenging situations and select the best choice regardless of whether the choice seems unpopular within the team. In short, the team leader needs both courage and good judgment to improve the outcomes of the team meeting.

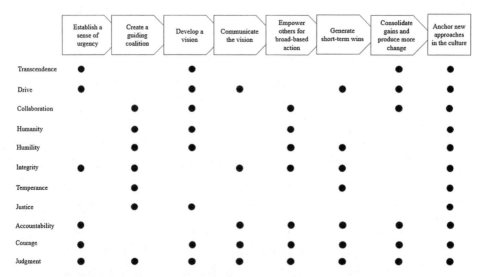

Figure 5.3 Characteristics and Functions of a Team Leader

Source: Seijts, G.H., & Gandz, J. (2018). Transformational change and leader character. *Business Horizons 61*(2), 239–249.

Becoming a Good Team Member

For members of a department to be labeled good team members, they need to demonstrate that they can successfully navigate high-stress situations without free-falling into the sympathetic state. The conflicts that emerged during Oliver's department meeting show that there is disunity within the department. Whether the team leader accuses the team members of not doing their fair share of work or of causing departmental issues, the team members throw allegations at one another, or both occur, the importance of good conflict-resolution strategies is clear. The emerging conflicts drove Oliver's team to the mobilization and immobilization states. To solve such a problem, the team members need to be educated on unity to effect conflict resolution.

Teams with members who have strong capabilities are more likely to work well together than those with low-ability members. These differences can be evaluated using cognitive or affective assessments. Similar to the team leader, team members are also characterized based on their reliance on the social engagement and sympathetic systems. However, team members are not as dependent on the sympathetic system as the team leaders are. Fundamentally, team members are individuals who have differing ideas and thought processes. Researchers label this unity of purpose as the "team mean."[7] A high team mean can increase the consensus between the members. However, it is also essential to understand that having a unified purpose and developing teams with similar characteristics does not automatically imply that the team will achieve the intended objectives. In other words, "birds of a feather may flock together, but that does not necessarily translate to confidence in the team."[8]

What this means is that cultivating high social affinity between the members does not necessarily indicate that the members will support each other to achieve the collective's goals.

Research shows that good teamwork is marked by cooperation, coordination, communication, conflict management, shared cognition, and coaching among the members.[9] These characteristics are essential for improving the outcomes of team activities as well as strengthening intergroup and intragroup relations. Therefore, it can be perceived that teams with members who possess these characteristics can achieve significant results in terms of improving the group's productivity.

Solving Team Problem by Applying the Polyvagal Theory

The breakdown in Oliver's department can be solved through proper leadership and conflict-resolution strategies. The two parties of the group encountered conflict due to the leader's flawed strategies and the members' poor communication. On one hand, Oliver isolated team members who delivered low performance, so his action was perceived as attacking those workers. On the other hand, the team members showed unnecessary aggression when discussing the issue. Perhaps Oliver felt that the burden of the department's low performance should have been placed on low-performing employees, or the team members felt that Oliver was wrongly blaming the members when the department's low performance should have been attributed to extenuating circumstances. Regardless of the root cause of the conflict, Oliver and his subordinates need to collaborate to reduce intergroup and intragroup conflict in his department.

To navigate conflict, the leader and team members can identify the triggers for transitioning across the different autonomic states of the Polyvagal Ladder. In Oliver's case, the group members were initially in the socialization state, but they gradually moved to the mobilization and immobilization states when Oliver started placing the blame on low-performing workers. Oliver and several department members shifted from the socialization state to the mobilization state. In addition, some members were stuck in the immobilization state due to their inability to respond to Oliver's accusations. Clearly, team conflict played a major role in the failure of the team meeting and the poor autonomic responses of the entire group. As you've learned, the three autonomic states are characterized by specific behaviors and emotional responses.[10] The socialization state includes elements of care and safety, whereas the mobilization state includes emotions and behaviors like anger, anxiety, and action. In contrast, the immobilization state results in collapse or loss of hope. If team leaders and members take these responses into consideration, they can mitigate intergroup conflict.

Mitigating conflict requires an understanding of how to recover to the social engagement state. For instance, the members in the mobilization state can be encouraged to regain calm with the use of safety cues, which we'll discuss soon, in order for them to participate in a mutually beneficial discussion. And, by also assuring the members in the immobilization state that they are in a safe environment, those workers can regain their ability to take action. As a result, it will be possible to encourage the workers, though they may still be in the sympathetic state, to provide valuable insights regarding the department's low performance.

One way to reduce the effects of the mobilization and immobilization states in workers is for the leader to provide a short, comforting intervention, such as communicating that the leader is grateful for the team's contributions even though the end result was not what they expected. For example, Oliver could say, "I am pleased with how hard you have been working, but there are a few changes we need to introduce to improve our overall performance. I would like everyone here to offer practical suggestions for improving productivity. Please feel free to share because you are in an open and safe environment." When coupled with other safety cues, including relaxed body language and facial expression, Oliver is able to communicate his opinions without shaming or triggering the mobilization and immobilization states among the team members.

Further Recommendations for Improving Group Synergy

While it's great for everyone to be aware of where they are on the Polyvagal Ladder so they can take active steps to reduce the chance of a conflict that gets out of hand and results in a communication breakdown and reduced productivity, actively training workers to handle conflict and drama in the workplace can result in a more harmonious and productive work environment. Moreover, providing an environment that feels safe, emotionally and psychologically, can result in workers who are effective, productive, and collaborative team members.

Train Teams to Resolve Conflict and Drama
in the Workplace

Conflict is often considered unavoidable in the organizational setting—or in any setting for that matter. Although different interventions can be used to prevent intergroup and intragroup conflict, the reality is that tension can emerge for trivial reasons as well as major ones. In *Polyvagal Exercises for Safety and Connection*, Deb Dana states, "We suffer when the people we care about are unable to meet us in the middle."[11] She points out that unintentional moments of disconnection often occur when a person perceives a discrepancy between their expectations (at a neural level) and the actual situation. These moments can manifest as micro moments or lingering experiences that create discomfort.[12]

The perceived discrepancies can be caused by mismatches in a group's relations, tasks, or processes, thereby amplifying the differences between group members.[13] These seemingly minor issues can build upon one another, potentially becoming an all-out conflict. And, if not promptly addressed, intergroup and intragroup conflict can cause various adverse consequences. Therefore, conflict-management training is a vital resource for encouraging workers to bridge the differences between their neural expectations of a situation and the actual situation.

Team training is a formalized structure for providing learning experiences with preset objectives and curricula to achieve specific team competencies.[14] The most common responses to team conflict are avoidance, forcing, yielding, and problem-solving, and you can guess which would likely be the most effective response. Therefore, team members require problem-solving strategies. While forcing, avoidance, and yielding can produce short-term results, these responses leave the team vulnerable to future conflicts[15] and potentially decreased productivity in the long run. Team members and group leaders must receive training that includes an understanding of the different types of organizational conflicts (see sidebar, "Types of Organizational Conflicts"). By dedicating adequate resources and support to professionals dealing with conflict, organizations can lessen the burden of conflict and simultaneously prevent conflicts from occurring in the future.

Types of Organizational Conflicts

In the *HBR Guide to Dealing with Conflict*, Amy Gallo sets forth four types of conflicts: (1) relationship conflict, (2) task conflict, (3) process conflict, and (4) status conflict.[16] Ranging from interpersonal issues and disagreements on the goals of a project to the best way to approach a task and, hey, who's in charge anyway—all of these conflicts have one factor in common: if they are not addressed when the conflict arises, it can send the affected team members (and even the organization) into a tailspin and disrupt productivity. While each of these conflicts presents in diverse ways and requires a targeted approach to resolution, an instinctive leader must be able to return to and/or remain in the socialization state and provide cues of safety (see next) to focus themselves and their team members on problem-solving strategies to remedy the conflict.

Provide Safety Cues to Mitigate Conflict and Drama

Cues of safety induce emotional and psychological safety in members of the organization. Williams explains that safety in the workplace is a neglected consideration because most researchers focus on *physical* safety, forgetting to stress the importance of psychological and emotional safety. For that reason, Williams claims that safety is a threefold approach to creating an inclusive work environment.[17] Emotional safety is essential for eliminating the triggers that induce stress and trauma, thereby preventing the worker from descending the Polyvagal Ladder. Emotional safety reflects the feeling of being protected from mental health issues that may emerge from a particular threat or event.[18]

In this context, psychological safety describes a worker's belief that the organizational context is safe, and it has minimal interpersonal risks for the employee. As a result, the employee develops capabilities for engaging in work-related activities without fear that they will suffer from negative consequences from their coworkers or superiors.[19] Research shows that the team leader's and the members' voices can play a major role in highlighting the level of psychological safety available in the workplace. While employees are usually attuned to the cues of safety evident in their immediate workplace, it is the managers and coworkers who are considered the leading parties in shaping the perceptions of safety.[20] To sum up, psychological safety can play a mediating role in the relationship between coworkers and supervisors.

Psychological and emotional safety is vital for improving the well-being of employees, increasing their productivity and overall satisfaction. The crux of emotional safety revolves around the feeling of being protected from internal and external influences that emerge in the surrounding work environment.[21] Accordingly, the worker gains the ability to characterize the influences based on the following dichotomies: good versus bad, safe versus dangerous, or comfortable versus uncomfortable.[22] The signals transmitted regarding the cues of safety or danger are essential for regulation and reaction to relevant stimuli related to safety or danger. The autonomic nervous system does not make judgments about good or bad; it simply focuses on managing risks in a manner that ensures the individual's safety.[23] The goal of emotional and psychological safety is to give the ventral vagal complex adequate resources to support prosocial behaviors aligned with the social engagement system.

We'll discuss more specifics regarding cues of safety in Chapters 6 and 7.

KEY POINTS

- An effective leader knows how to exercise good judgment and understands how to maneuver between the three autonomic states in the team setting.
- While in the socialization safe state, workers are engaged, collaborative, and productive.
- A leader's faulty approach and/or negative interaction between workers can put the team members in a sympathetic state, where productive communication is likely to take a nosedive.
- Depending on the members' levels of mobilization or immobilization, they may either argue or shut down, and it's up to the leader to help them return to a state where they can offer insight and problem-solving ideas.
- Constructing resilient teams involves training workers to handle conflict and providing cues of safety.

CHAPTER 6

Employee Motivation and the Polyvagal Theory

T he best strategies to motivate employees to be valuable team members often appeal to their personal motivations and preferences, at least in theory. The reality is, without an instinctive understanding of their personalities and ambitions, it can be quite challenging to ensure that employees are satisfied in their roles and in the workplace. In situations where employees sufficiently handle the same tasks and responsibilities on a daily basis, it's difficult to pinpoint when they are feeling dissatisfied or if they believe their responsibilities do not match their identities. Cultivating instinctive leadership helps a leader better relate to workers at both the personal and professional levels, bringing to light any issues so that change can be instituted. We'll begin this chapter by illustrating the importance of motivation in the workplace from Oliver Green's ongoing perspective. (He's currently feeling as if his employees just don't care.) Afterward, we'll describe how organizations can blend positive corporate cultures through evidence-based human resource strategies. By the end of this chapter, you should have a good understanding of why instinctive leadership is essential for building conducive work environments.

Oliver Green has been struggling to improve his department's performance. After his promotion, he was eager to interact with his employees because he believed he could revitalize the department. However, he adopted many strategies that failed. He alternated between leadership styles, finally settling on an approach that he believed was working. However, his department still recorded low productivity. In addition, the turnover rates in his department were increasingly higher than the values recorded in other departments. He reflected on this over the weekend and recognized that the motivation and retention problems were attributable to the workers' motivation rather than to his leadership strategy to approach each situation independently and respond accordingly. Oliver spent the following week evaluating his workers' behavior and noted several concerns regarding their daily habits:

Most team members seem easily distracted. They take frequent snack breaks and check their phones. A few even left the office to take personal calls.

Some are showing noticeable signs of exhaustion and frustration (yawning, slouching, and indifference) even though their workload is light.

General laxity is an issue for some, especially when they are handling activities that require movement between offices such as printing and delivering documents.

Some team members frequently report late, while others leave before the department's official closing hours. A few are daring enough to do both.

A few seem unnecessarily restless, even after completing their responsibilities for the day.

Oliver became more certain about his conclusion. Low motivation was a critical problem that he must address. Clearly, his employees were bored, but they weren't directly conveying their dissatisfaction to him. He wondered why. When he thought more about it, he realized that his employees were under a lot of stress; it had taken him a lot of time to find his footing as a leader. He suspected that fear of how he would react and perhaps other factors kept the workers from communicating their problems to him. Furthermore, he suspected that some employees felt unchallenged by their responsibilities, causing restlessness once their work had been completed. He'd heard a small group of workers grumbling to each other about how the organization did not offer sufficient benefits for their effort. They were the ones with low commitment. If these problems continue, Oliver fears his department will continue to lose vital personnel.

These conclusions raised a new set of challenges for Oliver: How do leaders motivate employees who have stopped caring?

Navigating Employee Boredom

Considerable research has been performed on the most effective methods for motivating employees. Some researchers claim that organizations should prioritize fulfilling the employees' extrinsic needs, while others highlight the need to appeal to the employees' intrinsic needs.[1] Kuvaas et al. found that when people are intrinsically motivated, organizations achieve better outcomes in terms of improving the employees' health and well-being. The same researchers state that the introduction of extrinsic motivation can actually undermine the organization's efforts to use intrinsic motivation strategies.[2] However, a select few researchers support the combination of both intrinsic and extrinsic motivation strategies.[3] These researchers make practical arguments about employee motivations. However, depending on the autonomic state an employee is in at any given time (that is, where they are on the Polyvagal Ladder), these motivations may not accurately reflect their needs, thereby impeding their satisfaction. In other words, the motivations that drive employee behaviors in the parasympathetic state may differ from the ones that emerge when they are in the sympathetic state.

Oliver's case makes it clear that there are scenarios in which a leader may experience challenging situations where their actions are unable to influence the employees' behaviors. These situations may compel the leader to feel helpless, but they also highlight weaknesses in the organization's human resource strategies. Considering that high employee motivation, commitment, and engagement levels are often associated with improved productivity,[4] it is essential for Oliver to determine how to improve the department's motivation levels. Ali et al. state that the process of organizational motivation usually begins with someone recognizing an unsatisfied need in the workplace that causes dissatisfaction or reduces the workers' engagement.[5] Accordingly, Oliver needs to take an active role in understanding the root causes of the employees' low motivation.

Using the Polyvagal Theory to Explain Low Employee Motivation

The department's issues can be traced to rational issues, such as intrinsic or extrinsic motivation. Otherwise, the low motivation can be traced to nonrational issues, such as the employee's transition between the sympathetic and parasympathetic states. For instance, mismatches between the employees' baseline autonomic state and their job descriptions can cause discrepancies in their behaviors and actions. We discussed this phenomenon in Chapter 3 using the examples of the business manager, frontline worker, and back-office worker. Due to differences in their baseline autonomic states, these people have unique behaviors and traits. Foremost, the business manager is more effective in the social engagement state. In comparison, the frontline worker has the ability to make good decisions in the mobilization state due to their resilience against stress and trauma. Last, the back-office workers are more effective in support roles because these roles often limit the workers' exposure to "extreme" external influences that cause mobilization and immobilization. Based on these roles, mismatches in the employees' job descriptions can reduce the employees' motivation in the workplace.

Organizational leaders need to acknowledge the cognitive traits that affect the work environment. As modern corporations strive to improve organizational productivity, the emphasis has gradually been shifting from the employees' needs to the organization's objectives. As a result, employees continue to experience adverse effects when organizations downsize or restructure.[6] With that said, emotionally intelligent leaders can recognize the employees' feelings, sentiments, and emotions. This rationale explains why emotionally intelligent leaders often have significant influence over the workers' performance. In this context, instinctive leadership, a skill that includes emotional intelligence, requires the leader to nurture rational and nonrational capabilities in a manner that inspires the workers to deliver optimal productivity in their respective professional roles. With an awareness of the general state of dissatisfaction among team members, a leader can apply the Polyvagal Theory to conventional motivation theories to create work environments that match the team members' baseline autonomic states and cultivate a satisfying work experience throughout the department or organization.

Motivating and Retaining Employees

To incorporate the Polyvagal Theory into the organizational setting, we will match its components with practical motivation theories: Maslow's hierarchy of needs and the job characteristics model. Maslow's motivation theory can explain why employees make decisions based on a hierarchy of needs. In addition, the theory highlights safety and security as vital components of employee motivation. The job characteristics model highlights the correlation between the workers' performance and their baseline autonomic responses. So, let's take a look at how leaders can apply the Polyvagal Theory to enhance their workers' motivation.

Hierarchy of Needs

Some team members in Oliver Green's department derive satisfaction when simple needs are fulfilled, but others have more demanding requirements. Oliver often struggles to identify the employees' needs because he believes that the workers are well compensated. In addition, they are allotted a good amount of personal time off and receive generous holiday benefits. He just cannot understand why so many employees are dissatisfied. In reality, many employees would prefer a promotion over tangible benefits, and while others do enjoy those benefits, some of them have been experiencing feelings of not being safe due to the high number of conflicts within the department. Evidently, Oliver needs to evaluate and classify his employees' needs to develop an appropriate response to the department's problems.

The hierarchy of needs is one of the most popular concepts for explaining the cognitive and affective factors surrounding employee motivation. The theory was conceptualized by Abraham Maslow in 1943.[7] According to this theory, human behavior is strongly dependent on the individual's needs. Maslow identified five key needs: physiological, safety, love and belonging, esteem, and self-actualization. The hierarchy of these needs is illustrated by a five-layered pyramid. Maslow refers to the first four layers as "deficiency layers." If these needs are not fulfilled, they may cause tension, anxiety, or other adverse effects in an individual. Accordingly, these four needs must be fulfilled before the individual pursues the need at the top of the pyramid: self-actualization. For that reason, human beings have an instinctive desire to fulfill the needs in the deficiency layers before pursuing the cherry on top: self-actualization. Failure to fulfill these needs can drive a person to experience extreme states that may push them toward mobilization or immobilization. Figure 6.1 illustrates the hierarchy of needs specifically with regard to employees.

In our culture, a need for food, water, shelter, and warmth is relatively easy to fulfill. Feeling secure, stable, and safe is a little more difficult, but it is still usually within reach. As you can see, the higher you go on the pyramid, the more difficult it is to fulfill a need. If an employee's needs are not met in any one of these deficiency layers in the workplace, their motivation and commitment will usually falter. The level at which an employee's needs are met in each of these areas will directly affect their level of satisfaction at work, as illustrated by Figure 6.2.

Figure 6.1 Hierarchy of Employee Needs

Source: Wright, T. (2023, August 1). Maslow's Hierarchy as a Business Framework, Cascade, https://www.cascade.app/blog/maslows-hierarchy

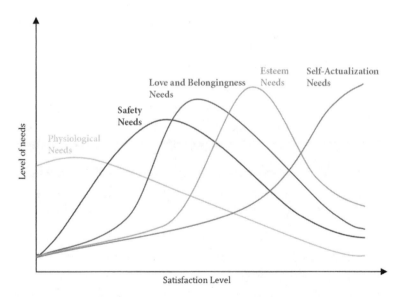

Figure 6.2 The Relationship Between Needs and Satisfaction

Source: Tezcan, U., Sibel, A., & Emine, G. (2017). Maslow's Hierarchy of Needs in 21st Century: The Examination of Vocational Differences. In Uysal, H. T., Aydemir, S., and Genç, E. (Eds.), *Researches on Science and Art in 21st-century Turkey 1*, 211–227.

The physiological needs correspond with the primary needs, whereas safety and security focus on the person's stability and protection.[8] In the workplace, physiological needs include financial compensation, food, air conditioning/heat, and other environmental needs. Safety and security are more reflective of the Polyvagal Theory because the human body is naturally designed to respond to cues of danger and safety. This response is genetically and neurobiologically ingrained in the human body. With regard to love and belonging, this dimension focuses on the employees' desires for affection, such as recognition from their peers, superiors, and customers.[9] Consequently, self-esteem deals with the employees' achievement, competence, and perceived recognition in the workplace. This esteem is attributed to the workers' respect for themselves and others in the workplace. In the end, the final need is self-actualization. Self-actualization is often considered the most difficult need to fulfill because of its position in the hierarchy.[10]

To reiterate, research shows that the hierarchy of needs begins with the pursuit of primitive needs (physiological needs), and when those needs are fulfilled, then the person gradually begins to pursue less vital needs, such as esteem and ultimately self-actualization.[11] Clearly, Maslow's theory corresponds with the Polyvagal Theory in terms of explaining the hierarchical nature of human behavior.

In this context, the focus is placed on the employees' safety and security needs. Safety and security needs can be identified based on the individual's perceptions of danger and safety. For example, safety can represent an employee's viewpoint toward shelter, protection, or harm.[12] In other words, a person can feel safe because they are in a safe environment or because a guardian is present. In comparison, danger cues are more abstract because they encompass a wide variety of situations: risk of poverty, exposure to danger, or a legal situation.[13] These situations may cause the person to shift to the mobilization or immobilization state, depending on their severity. Although some of these events are not practical in organizational settings, it can be perceived that exposure to extreme situations of stress, anger, or anxiety can skew a person's autonomic nervous system to respond to danger. In brief, employees often feel safe when their basic needs are fulfilled.

Job Characteristics

Recently, Oliver has dedicated a lot of time and effort to trying to better understand his employees. Despite this effort, his workers are still clearly dissatisfied. After several one-on-one discussions, Oliver comes to understand that some of his employees would like the opportunity to change positions—some workers feel that their tasks have become monotonous, others feel that they lack autonomy, and a small group, especially more recent workers, claim they do not receive enough feedback. Oliver now knows that these are the issues that have caused a decline in the workers' commitment and overall performance. His most important task now is to assess how to provide employees with jobs that match their unique traits and professional needs.

The Job Characteristics Model explains that certain job characteristics are aligned with varying psychological states. This model was conceptualized in the 1980s by Greg Hackman and Richard Oldham to explain the relationship between job characteristics and employees' responses at work. The model sets forth five key job characteristics: skill variety, task identity, task significance, autonomy, and feedback.[14] The theory behind the model proposes that organizations can create engaging and meaningful work environments by altering these dimensions in accordance with the employees' tastes and preferences. In other words, organizations can increase employee motivation by creating job descriptions that are segmented based on these traits or recruiting workers who accurately reflect these traits. If the organization fails to create this match, the employees may more easily shift down the Polyvagal Ladder. If the organization is effective at creating this match by taking the necessary steps, it will cause profound changes in the employees' satisfaction level and overall productivity.

Basically, the Job Characteristics Model highlights a strong relationship between job attributes and employees' psychological outcomes. As shown in Figure 6.3, the five attributes of job characteristics have direct relationshps with employee responsibility, meaningfulness, and knowledge of results.[15] The figure illustrates that these dimensions have significant influence on employees' motivation and job satisfaction.

The five job characteristics reflect different dimensions of conventional organizational positions.

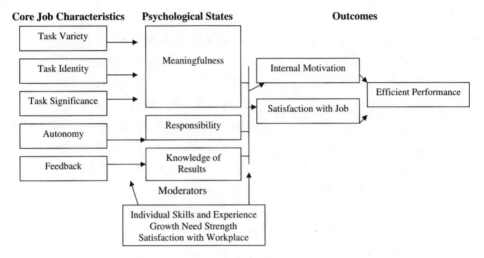

Figure 6.3 Relationship Between Job Characteristics and Employee Psychological State

Source: Mayrowetz, D., Murphy, J., Seashore Louis, K., & Smylie, M.A. (2007). Distributed leadership as work redesign: Retrofitting the job characteristics model, *Leadership and Policy in Schools* 6(1), 69–101.

- **Task or skill variety** describes the extent to which a specific job requires different skills and talents.[16] This consideration reflects the level of independence and responsibility experienced by workers.
- **Task identity** refers to the degree to which a job requires completion of an entire task with visible outcomes.
- **Task significance** explains the degree to which the job has a significant impact on people in the immediate organization or in the world at large.
- **Autonomy** describes whether the employee can work independently within a job.
- **Feedback** explains whether the employee receives accurate and effective information regarding their role.[17]

Organizations must ensure that these job characteristics match the employees' preferences to ensure that they are motivated for their respective roles and responsibilities.

The Job Characteristics Model can also be used to explain the behaviors of leaders and followers in complex organizational settings. In the modern business environment, it is well known that positive psychological states correlate with high motivation and work performance. However, it is also widely acknowledged that certain job characteristics can cause distress and mental health problems in the workplace.[18] Considering that most employees spend prolonged periods at work, we can easily hypothesize that employees' job environment has a substantial impact on their psychological state. Furthermore, adverse psychological states can worsen work performance and increase burnout among workers.[19] In other cases, it can actually encourage the employee to turn to destructive coping mechanisms. Therefore, evidence-based research underscores the importance of creating conducive work environments that support employees, based partly on their characteristics.

Enhancing the Staff's Sense of Purpose and Meaning

What we can determine from the discussion of Maslow's theory and Hackman and Oldham's model is that employee motivation is based on a hierarchy of needs as it relates to job characteristics as well as the work environment. These needs represent the intrinsic and extrinsic sources of motivation in the workplace. Failure to fulfill physiological, safety, love and belonging, and esteem needs can drive a person into the fight-or-flight response in a struggle to get those needs met. Likewise, discrepancies between job characteristics and the employee's traits can also cause adverse changes in the person's autonomic state.

When these concepts are integrated with the Polyvagal Theory, leaders can understand the importance of utilizing strategies that appeal to the employees' intrinsic and extrinsic needs in a manner that reduces stress and other negative emotions. The fulfillment of needs is essential for creating cues of safety that support social engagement rather than mobilization and immobilization in the workplace.

The leader plays a vital role in guiding the organization's culture and vision. Low organizational motivation creates negative psychological states that are detrimental to overall productivity. In the current environment, a popular ideology has emerged that the growth of corporations is primarily dependent on their financial pools rather than on their human resources.[20] Although this ideology is relatively true, it often misleads organizations to prioritize financial drivers of performance over human factors. Therefore, leaders need to understand how to balance the employees' needs and the capabilities and demands of the organization.[21] This balance is essential for driving the employees to support the organization's vision. This goal can be achieved by encouraging the workers to support a unified work vision that exudes commitment, loyalty, and engagement.

Continuous deprivation of the employees' intrinsic and extrinsic needs can reduce employee retention rates and amplify turnover intentions. In simple cases, poor work environments and the deprivation of employee rewards causes dissatisfaction and low engagement. In extreme scenarios, these environments can encourage the workers to leave the organization. On top of losing essential workers, organizations may also experience losses or declines in their financial productivity.[22] Employee turnover is usually caused by discrepancies between the job and the person, but it can also be triggered by stress, lack of career advancement opportunities, low trust, personnel conflicts, ineffective human resource policies, or work overload.[23] Among these problems, Oliver's department was struggling with both low motivation and poor communication. Low motivation emerged due to the lack of career advancement opportunities and poor mismatch between the employees' baseline autonomic state and their job characteristics. These issues explain the employees' high laxity and lateness, as well as their low commitment and engagement levels.

With regard to poor communication, this problem emerges due to mistrust between the employees and the leaders. Research shows that various leadership styles can enhance trust between the leader and the followers. For example, Men et al. outlined that the transformational and servant leadership styles are particularly designed to build trust in the workplace.[24] Trust becomes particularly important during turbulent times. Researchers used the global pandemic to explain the value of good supervisory communication and trust in organizational outcomes.[25] Nonetheless, trust and communication are difficult to build, especially when the employees are in a sympathetic state or in parasympathetic shutdown due to extreme fear, stress, or anger. Given that mobilization and immobilization often adversely affect behavior, it should be clear that trust and communication are integral for strengthening social engagement and helping employees recover from these states. Oliver Green needs to use motivation strategies that simultaneously improve his subordinates' satisfaction while also supporting social engagement within the department.

Applying the Polyvagal Theory to Strengthen Employees' Sense of Purpose and Meaning

In alignment with the Polyvagal Theory, leaders need to understand how different motivation strategies affect the employees' autonomic state and overall satisfaction at work. Foremost, the leader needs to create measures that target the employees' primitive needs: physiological needs, safety and security, love and belonging, and esteem. This strategy is vital for creating a safe environment that encourages the workers to shift from the sympathetic state back to the ventral parasympathetic state.

Oliver can achieve this goal by providing fundamental tangible and intangible benefits to the workers. This strategy will encourage the workers to shift their focus from instinctive needs to the more critical needs of esteem and self-actualization, where the employee's full potential can be realized. Oliver also needs to identify mismatches between employees' traits and their job characteristics. Among his subordinates, several showed clear dissatisfaction with their work responsibilities, and others revealed that they were open to new career opportunities. These recommendations address the workers' intrinsic and extrinsic needs and also offer Oliver the opportunity to create a conducive environment for improving staff communication.

Employee Motivation and Retention Strategies

The resolution of the motivation problem that Oliver was experiencing required a multifaceted strategy that focused on improving both employee satisfaction and communication. Complementary or alternative strategies could also help Oliver achieve his goal of improving employee motivation and work performance. These include balancing intrinsic and extrinsic motivation, providing cues of safety, and blending appropriate corporate cultures. Let's consider each.

Balancing Intrinsic and Extrinsic Motivation

Oliver needs to balance intrinsic and extrinsic rewards to strengthen the department's performance. By placing too much emphasis on extrinsic rewards (monetary rewards and employee benefits), Oliver may neglect to provide adequate intrinsic rewards to workers (employee recognition and inspiration). Therefore, Oliver needs to identify whether each employee's low satisfaction level stems from the lack of intrinsic or extrinsic rewards. With that done, Oliver will develop a suitable equilibrium of intrinsic and extrinsic rewards in the department.

Intrinsic and extrinsic motivation strategies are the most fundamental remedy for optimizing employee motivation and reducing turnover intentions. Reliable research explains that determining whether an employee is motivated by intrinsic or extrinsic motivation is vital for performance and growth.[26] All employees are drawn to organizations because of intrinsic motivation, extrinsic motivation, or a combination of both components of motivation. This rationale applies in both personal and professional settings.[27] The two motivation components appeal to different aspects of a worker's psychological and emotional state. Intrinsic motivation is more effective than extrinsic motivation in terms of optimizing work performance, but extrinsic motivation often carries more weight in the organizational landscape depending on the type of work setting.[28] Therefore, motivation issues can be eliminated by evaluating whether employees prefer intrinsic motivation through intangible benefits or extrinsic motivation through tangible rewards.

Instead of selecting between intrinsic and extrinsic motivation, the leader can merge the two motivation theories to determine a suitable equilibrium that appeals to the employees' personal and professional goals. As mentioned earlier, some researchers argue that intrinsic and extrinsic motivation are inseparable, and others claim that they compete with each for dominance.[29] In other words, it is impossible to offer intrinsic motivation without affecting extrinsic motivation, and vice versa. In this context, the balance between intrinsic and extrinsic motivation can be determined by evaluating the employees' responses to rewards and punishments. In Oliver's case, the provision of intrinsic rewards (employee recognition) and extrinsic rewards (career advancement opportunities) would play a vital role in creating positive relationships with his subordinates. Other rewards such as bonuses, paid time off, training opportunities, and similar perks can be integrated into the strategy without adversely affecting employee satisfaction.

Providing Cues of Safety

Assuring employees that they are safe with the use of safety cues encourages them to remain in the socialization state. The deprivation of intrinsic and extrinsic needs and mistrust between Oliver and his subordinates contributed significantly to the department's low motivation. Oliver was unaware of the struggles his employees were experiencing. From his perspective, the workers were lazy and noncooperative, as illustrated by their laxity and low commitment to their respective responsibilities. Oliver felt that his workers did not care about his authority, their performance, or the department's objectives. However, the reality was that the employees did not feel safe confiding in their leader. As a result, the workers grew accustomed to their daily routines regardless of Oliver's concerns. Therefore, Oliver needed to provide cues of safety to encourage the workers to convey their opinions regarding any issues in the department.

As we've discussed, the human autonomic nervous system relies on passive pathways of neuroception to evaluate whether the surrounding environment is conducive to social engagement.[30] Because this occurs beneath conscious awareness, a person may not even recognize that their environment is causing them to feel unsafe. In fact, the human mind usually pursues cues of safety and danger even before employees arrive at their destination.[31] Accordingly, leaders need to understand how to use cues of safety to encourage employees to perceive the environment as safe in order for them to remain in the socialization state. Simple gestures, body language, and vocal behaviors can regulate the response of the workers' autonomic nervous system. Additionally, the surrounding space can be altered to create positive feelings among the workers (there's more on this in Chapter 7). These cues of safety can be integrated into Oliver's leadership strategy, into the department's communication strategies, and into the work environment.

Blending Corporate Culture Styles

According to research, there are various styles of corporate culture, which have been refined down to purpose, caring, safety, learning, results, enjoyment, authority, and order.[32] These corporate culture styles are oriented toward pursuing different organizational objectives. Each has a separate focus and attributes, which can be deduced from their labels. However, there are more intricate considerations to take into account that go beyond the scope of this work. Nevertheless, the concept of blending corporate culture styles is a valid strategy to meet the various needs of employees.

In Oliver's case, his department's motivation issues emerged because the workers were unable to reach an agreement with their leader about their preferred sources of motivation, job characteristics, and communication strategies. To address these issues, Oliver felt a blending of corporate culture styles made sense: he would take his team's opinions into consideration when making decisions regarding the department. Because fear and mistrust were major concerns that prevented the workers from communicating their opinions regarding Oliver's leadership and motivation strategies, he would ensure that his team felt safe when communicating with him. Accordingly, blending the corporate culture styles would allow Oliver to strengthen communication and transparency in the workplace, among other benefits.

The integration of safety in an organization requires the leader and the employees to view it as an integral component of day-to-day operations rather than as a separate function.[33] This recommendation will allow Oliver to create a work culture that reflects the needs and preferences of the workers while also strengthening the department's productivity.

KEY POINTS

- Leaders need to recognize that some situations cannot be resolved by changing their leadership approach. In such situations, the leader needs to evaluate the employees' sources of motivation and their corresponding psychological and autonomic states.
- Maslow's hierarchy of needs explains that an employee's intrinsic needs follow a systematic hierarchy that determines their overall satisfaction levels.
- The Job Characteristics Model focuses on the workers' environment and the correlation of extrinsic work characteristics.
- Discrepancies between the employees' desires and job characteristics can lower their motivation and satisfaction levels. If the problem worsens, the organization may experience rising turnover rates.
- The Polyvagal Theory elucidates that the leader needs to match the organization's motivation strategies to the workers' needs and job characteristics to ensure that the motivational approaches align with the workers' preferences.
- Complementary strategies for improving the workers' satisfaction levels include balancing intrinsic and extrinsic motivation, providing cues of safety, and blending corporate culture styles.

CHAPTER 7

Cultivating Instinctive Leadership for a Steadfast Foundation

Now that you have a good understanding of how the Polyvagal Theory applies to employee behavior and overall outcomes in the workplace and how to apply its lessons to challenges in departments and organizations, let's look at it as a road map for cultivating instinctive leadership. In this chapter, we'll narrow down the attributes and skills leaders need to use to strengthen their rational and nonrational decision-making capabilities in the organizational setting. Afterward, we'll illuminate how leaders can navigate through obstacles that emerge from their interactions with different organizational groups, such as customers and supervisors. Finally, we'll clarify how the instinctive leader can set up the surrounding physical environment to strengthen social engagement. Overall, we'll summarize how leaders can maintain a stable autonomic state to improve their interactions with others and enhance their decision-making capabilities. To begin the journey of instinctive leadership, leaders need to understand their own strengths and weaknesses, so let's take that first step now.

When Oliver Green was promoted to senior executive, he was eager to prove himself to his supervisors, his team, and himself. While his knowledge and expertise allowed him to maneuver through the usual daily obstacles and engage with his subordinates, he struggled with many of his new responsibilities. His problems reached a crescendo with the declining productivity of his department's workers. Though Oliver eventually found his footing thanks to what he learned about instinctive leadership and the Polyvagal Theory, during his struggles he was finding it difficult to get going in the mornings, fearing the day would hold more of the same: overwhelming stress. Even when he tried to greet the day with renewed enthusiasm, he'd find himself frozen in place when faced with making a decision. *Is this the right decision? Will it result in loss? Will an unexpected issue arise as a result of this choice? What don't I know that will impact the outcome?*

If you've been following along with Oliver all this time, you know that his stock trading decisions were negatively affected and that some of his staff felt he had become increasingly biased, others complained he'd become ornery and short-tempered, and others felt like he just didn't understand them. Oliver knew he needed more time to gain his footing, but time was his most limited resource. Instinctive leadership and complementary strategies were the answer to help Oliver overcome the mounting stress caused by his daily responsibilities. In this way, he could move forward from a more relaxed state and start making good decisions, taking into account both rational and nonrational thought processes.

Numerous factors can hamper performance and relationships between workers in an organizational environment and impact a leader's ability to keep operations running smoothly. An instinctive leader often needs to make quick judgments using existing information and intuition. This requires being able to regulate their autonomic state to ensure that these decisions are made in an optimal state.

Learning instinctive leadership is a process that involves two steps: nurturing intuitive intelligence and maintaining an optimal autonomic state. These steps do not occur overnight. Rather, they require strategic implementation to improve leadership outcomes and overall productivity over time. Let's consider what's involved with each.

Nurturing Intuitive Intelligence

Intuitive intelligence is a vital aspect of instinctive leadership that allows the leader to make optimal decisions, even during times of distress. While analytical decision-making is the conventional approach used by most leaders and often makes the most sense when all the information is available and time is not of the essence, intuition is particularly useful for times when all factors cannot be known. In both scenarios, the instinctive leader needs to understand the inherent strengths and weaknesses of both approaches to decide how to respond to a particular situation for the most successful outcome.

In reality, there are many situations where the leader's decision may be hampered by constraints in their internal or external environment. Leadership is a natural and spontaneous process that allows one to create meaning in the organization and encourage workers to support a common goal.[1] Although this ideology has been criticized by scientific scholars, intuitive leadership can play a major role by encouraging leaders to use their somatic awareness and conscious minds to improve the outcomes of their choices.[2] Overall, the cultivation of instinctive leadership requires a leader to have an open mind to more accurately identify the state of their autonomic nervous system (and hence their mental faculties) in any given moment and utilize the skills to shift to the more desired state, if needed. This intuitive intelligence allows leaders to be more flexible and adaptive in their daily decisions and interactions with others without being triggered into a state of aggression or withdrawal.

Although research regarding instinctive leadership is scarce, some individuals have published articles that provide significant information regarding intuition and instinctive leadership. For instance, the founder of Oxford Leadership, Brian Bacon, claimed that a vast majority of leaders reject instinctive leadership because they feel it has little or no function in the business setting.[3] The scholar criticized this belief by explaining that intuition is a vital dimension of leadership, as follows:

> Can you think of an occasion where you've had a gut feeling that something wasn't right about a significant business issue but didn't listen to your intuition and later regretted it? Do you often doubt your intuition in favor of hard evidence to support your business decisions? If so, you may be underutilizing one of the most powerful leadership tools, your intuitive intelligence.[4]

Bacon proposes that intuition is more than a gut feeling. Significant research performed into the origins of intuition reveals that intuition manifests due to the brain's ability to piece together information from a person's surroundings, experiences, and options.[5] Instinctive leadership relies on the use of both analytic and instinctive cognitive faculties to make outstanding choices. While IQ and emotional intelligence are relatively important in the organizational setting, however, the reality is that intuitive intelligence is a skill that has been neglected by many leaders.

Intuitive Intelligence Helps Oliver Solve His Problem

In Oliver's case, instinctive leadership requires him to rely on different mental faculties to improve his decision-making during good and bad times. By relying on a combination of his knowledge, emotions, and intuitive intelligence, Oliver can make optimal decisions that are more immune to bias. To achieve this goal, he needs to identify whether his daily challenges demand rational thought, nonrational thought, or a combination of the two. For instance, departmental issues such as low productivity can be addressed using analytical strategies. Oliver can incorporate appropriate strategies to understand what motivates his workers. In comparison, some problems require intuitive approaches. For example, Oliver may be compelled to rely on intuition to better understand his employees' perceptions. By placing too much focus on rational decision-making, he may have neglected his intuitive intelligence as a valuable tool for resolving various organizational issues.

Maintaining an Optimal Autonomic State

As you now understand, instinctive leadership involves the use of both rational and nonrational mental faculties to improve decision-making. However, it is unrealistic to expect leaders to always make accurate intuitive decisions, especially when they are under stress. During such situations, leaders need to recalibrate their autonomic state to increase accuracy and reduce errors caused by bias and other influences. The methods for maintaining the optimal autonomic state include overriding the body's response through the "vagal brake," creating a tailored profile map, tracking triggers that change one's autonomic state, and adopting evidence-based regulation skills. These methods rely on different mechanisms to give the leader the opportunity to make effective judgments. Let's take a look at each.

Exercising the Vagal Brake

The vagal brake is the right vagus nerve, which connects to the heart.[6] One of the most important functions of the vagal brake is to regulate the heart's pacemaker to promote the outcomes of a safe state.[7] When the vagal brake achieves its function, it can alleviate the body's response to external challenges, keeping an individual from succumbing to the mobilization or immobilization state by encouraging the body to remain calm. When the vagal brake is dysfunctional, an individual's threshold to negative cues may be adversely altered,[8] heightening the fight, flight, or freeze response in the face of non-life-threatening situations. This line of reasoning highlights the importance of the Polyvagal Theory as it applies to regulating a leader's susceptibility to stress and other negative emotional influences. The good news is that the vagal brake can be strengthened with targeted exercises. Clearly, Oliver Green was in dire need of a stronger vagal brake to keep him showing up at the office, navigating his many challenges, and making decisions he felt good about.

The vagal brake can be exercised in individual and group contexts to improve engagement in the organizational setting. Flores and Porges outline that exercising the vagal brake can provide repeated opportunities for team members to maneuver through different autonomic states.[9] They say, "Just as going to the gym to work out regularly improves muscle tone through doing push-ups and sit-ups, a good workout of the social engagement system in a group strengthens the vagal brake."[10] In other words, the researchers explain that exercising the vagal brake can allow a leader to modulate emotional and psychological states depending on the surrounding stimuli. As a result, exercising the vagal brake can eventually improve the leader's ability to engage and disengage with other parties. Methods to build this capacity include mindfulness and vocalization (especially singing) exercises. Exercising the vagal brake is a test of one's resilience to allow the individual to override defensive states in line with their objectives, much like weightlifting is the test of one's strength with the overall goal of getting stronger over time.

Exercising the Vagal Brake Helps Oliver Solve His Problem

Oliver isn't much of a singer. In fact, his singing has been described as monotonous and tense, so he usually just hums quietly along in group song. Fortunately, mindfulness *is* something he can do to exercise the vagal brake to build resiliency against organizational issues. As Oliver's work responsibilities increased, his stress and anxiety levels increased correspondingly. Therefore, he needed to take control of his psychological state in a manner that would allow him to cope with emerging issues. Having an optimally functioning vagus brake would encourage him to report to work with a more positive outlook even with the understanding that the day would hold many challenges. By remaining calm during times of distress, Oliver would be able to make decisions with confidence and drastically improve the outcomes.

Drawing a Personal Autonomic Map

"Mapping the nervous system" is another strategy for improving the regulation of an individual's psychological state. In *Polyvagal Exercises for Safety and Connection*, Deb Dana explains that the mapping process can allow a person to cultivate a habit of autonomic awareness by tracking what leads the person from one state to another. Although the Polyvagal Ladder illustrates how a person can transition across different autonomic states, it does not provide a means of assessing the person's short-term and long-term trajectory. Correspondingly, autonomic maps can be utilized to create a habit of understanding so that a person can easily monitor their position in the autonomic hierarchy. In addition, being able to visually recognize one's state of regulation or dysregulation can have a powerful impact on the individual's neurobiological response. The human mind is inherently attentive to visual cues. For instance, every culture has its own maps that are shared or communicated between individuals. In a similar sense, the autonomic map can be used to guide employees to return to the safety of the ventral vagal state.

Several maps have been designed to monitor a person's autonomic state. In this context, we will focus on three interrelated maps with different objectives designed by Dana and presented in the aforementioned book:

1. **Personal Profile Map.** This map seeks to answer "Where am I?" It provides a foundational explanation of the person's position in the autonomic hierarchy.
2. **Triggers and Glimmers Map.** This map can offer unique insights into a person's triggers by asking,

"What brought me here?" This question requires the person to identify triggers that compel them to shift to the sympathetic or dorsal vagal state, as well as glimmers that strengthen their social engagement system.

3. **Regulating Resources Map.** This map is classified as the final mapping sequence because it encourages the individual to ask, "How do I find my way to ventral vagal regulation?"

These questions are designed to map an individual's journey back to the socialization state. Foremost, the Personal Profile Map is designed to analyze one's autonomic awareness in a manner that enlightens them about relevant neuroception characteristics. As a result, the map can be used to anchor the person's position in the autonomic hierarchy. The map not only identifies the individual's autonomic state but also allows the person to safely activate the sympathetic and dorsal states without being hijacked by mobilization or immobilization.[11]

The Personal Profile Map

The Personal Profile Map consists of three write-in areas that correspond with the key stages of the autonomic hierarchy, as shown in Figure 7.1. The person may use different colors to reflect their perceptions of the autonomic states—for example, yellow for calm, red for stress, and blue for shutdown. For the top section correlating to the ventral vagal socialization state, the person is encouraged to remember a time when they felt safe and imagine the feelings that emerged due to the surrounding energy. They are then invited to write how they feel in that state and how the world seems to them.

With regard to the sympathetic mobilization state, the person needs to think about situations in which they feel unsafe or overwhelmed. They would then note how they feel and how the world seems to them. With regard to the final dorsal vagal state of immobilization, the person imagines scenarios where they feel disconnected at work or experience a situation of collapse. They would then similarly note how they feel and how they perceive the world when in that state.

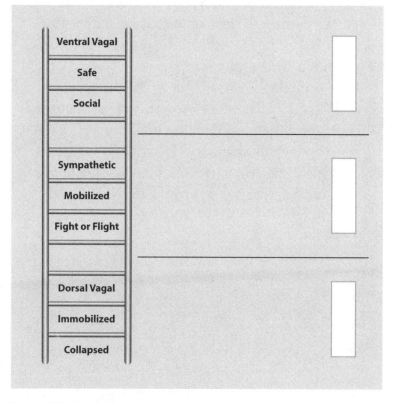

Figure 7.1 The Personal Profile Map

Source: Dana, D. (2018, p. 64). *The Polyvagal Theory in Therapy: Engaging the Rhythm of Regulation> (Norton Series on Interpersonal Neurobiology).* WW Norton & Company.

Oliver's Personal Profile Map

Oliver began his position as senior executive in the safety state, which he identifies as the color yellow (Figure 7.2). In the face of mounting challenges, he transitioned to mobilization (which he identifies as red) and then to immobilization (which he identifies as blue). At first, Oliver was eager to accept his responsibilities, so he used social engagement to try to improve the department's staff relationships. However, his work struggles exhausted him to the extent that he started fearing going into the office. This issue reflects his transition to the mobilization state through the fight-or-flight response. In some cases, Oliver avoids making decisions because he fears that the choices will have detrimental implications on the department's productivity. Clearly, Oliver's psychological state is erratic based on how frequently he transitions across the three autonomic states.

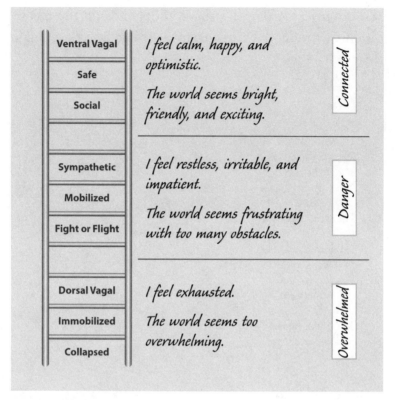

Figure 7.2 Oliver's Personal Profile Map

The Triggers and Glimmers Map

The Triggers and Glimmers Map (Figure 7.3), which looks very much like the template for the Personal Profile Map with the exception of the labels in the write-in sections, is particularly suitable for analyzing the root causes of changes in a person's autonomic state. This map primarily focuses on the factors that lead to moments of activation or regulation using triggers or glimmers. Fundamentally, triggers describe the cues of danger that activate the body's defense states through the sympathetic or dorsal pathways.[12] Contrarily, glimmers clarify the cues of safety aligned with health, healing, and growth.[13] A person's survival depends on the recognition of productive and harmful influences that shape their behaviors.

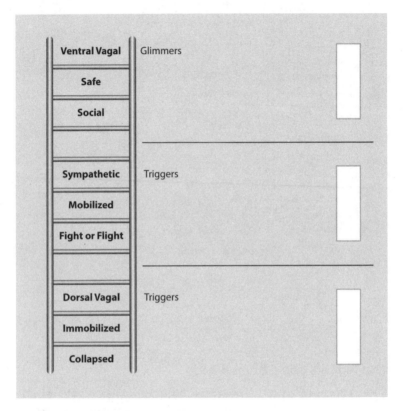

Figure 7.3 The Triggers and Glimmers Map

Source: Dana, D. (2018, p. 72). *The Polyvagal Theory in Therapy: Engaging the Rhythm of Regulation (Norton Series on Interpersonal Neurobiology).* WW Norton & Company.

Oliver's Triggers and Glimmers Map

In Oliver's case, he can identify his glimmers and triggers to understand the causes of his behavioral changes at work (Figure 7.4). Foremost, the most evident glimmer revolves around Oliver's professional recognition. When Oliver was promoted to senior executive, he felt that the organization recognized his contributions, thereby allowing him to feel calm and safe during his initial days after the promotion. Afterward, overwhelming stress at work pushed him to the mobilization state, as seen by his reluctance to go to work on most mornings. As time went on, overwhelming fear pushed him to the immobilization state by making him freeze when making major decisions.

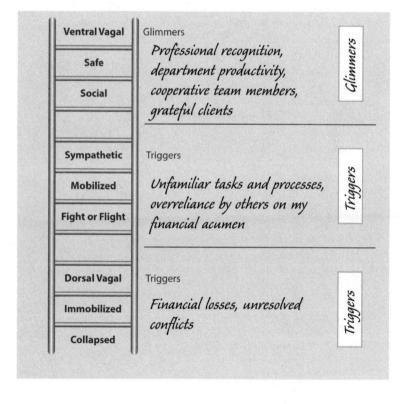

Figure 7.4 Oliver's Triggers and Glimmers Map

The Regulating Resources Map

The final step of autonomic mapping involves the use of the Regulating Resources Map (Figure 7.5) to push one's autonomic state toward the socialization state. This map is designed to evaluate individual and group measures that can be used to achieve regulation and prevent the individual from succumbing to their defense states. The map is aligned with the triggers and glimmers. For instance, the person can strengthen glimmers by asking, "What helps me stay here?" In comparison,

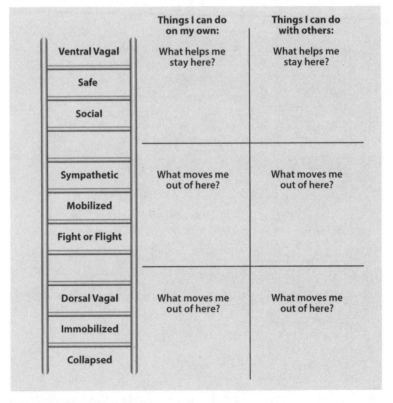

Figure 7.5 The Regulating Resources Map

Source: Dana, D. (2018, p. 79). *The Polyvagal Theory in Therapy: Engaging the Rhythm of Regulation (Norton Series on Interpersonal Neurobiology).* WW Norton & Company.

the triggers can be evaluated by asking, "What moves me out of here?" These questions are the backbone of the map because they offer insights into a variety of effective regulation strategies that can be used individually and/or in group settings.

Oliver's Regulating Resources Map

Oliver can use his Regulating Resources Map to regulate his behaviors at work to optimize his own and his department's productivity (Figure 7.6). Several recommendations can be made to improve Oliver's psychological state. For instance, Oliver can focus on his personal and professional recognition to strengthen his socialization state. By himself, Oliver derives a lot of satisfaction from personal and professional recognition. However, group settings require Oliver to strive to be recognized by different individuals: superiors, work colleagues, and subordinates. He can also use regulation skills such as mindfulness and breathing techniques to move his system toward a more ventral vagal state. With regard to Oliver's tendency to want to "flee" the workplace (or avoid it entirely), he can leave this state by identifying unique and meaningful reasons to go to work in the morning. He can also rely on his social interactions to return to a calm state. Finally, Oliver can leave the immobilization state by developing appropriate methods for resolving organizational issues, including reaching out to others for support and gently guiding his nervous system toward more energy and activity. In group situations, Oliver is encouraged to collaborate with other personnel to reduce the fear of making bad decisions.

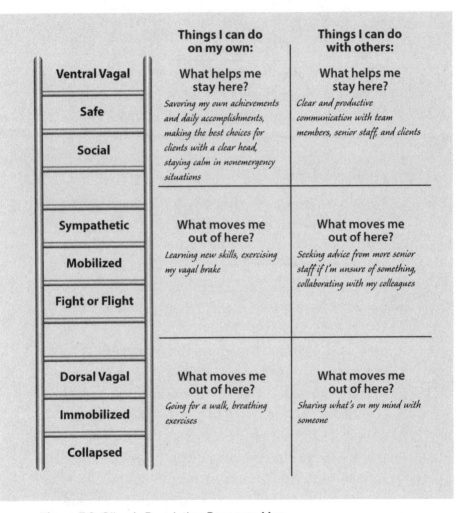

Figure 7.6 Oliver's Regulating Resource Map

Learning and Cultivating Regulation Skills

Instinctive leaders can learn to shift their bodies to the socialization state by using certain skills as soon as they notice that they are descending the Polyvagal Ladder. Because the autonomic nervous system is designed to dampen sympathetic activation in safe environments and "safety trumps fear,"[14] when we take active steps to cue our bodies that we are safe, our bodies respond accordingly.

Regulation skills, which include exercising the vagal brake, fall into two categories: conventional or nonconventional. Conventional strategies include evidence-based approaches such as breathing techniques, eye and body movements, orienting attention, vocalization, and grounding meditation, as described below. Nonconventional strategies often lie outside Western conventions, such as tai chi, yoga, or martial arts.[15] While these methods rely on different mechanisms, they are oriented toward strengthening the relationships between the brain, mind, and body. We'll describe some of these skills now, but this is not an exhaustive list or a comprehensive overview, as a complete discussion of these skills and techniques goes beyond the scope of this book.

Breathing Techniques

Because the transition across different autonomic states is reflected by changes in a person's breathing patterns, breathing techniques can play a vital role in providing appropriate stimuli for regulating an individual's psychological state. Research shows that breathing and emotions are bidirectional stimuli; hence, each emotional state corresponds with a particular breathing pattern.[16] For instance, slow breathing strategies can reduce the overactivity of the vagal components of the central nervous system and improve cognitive functions.[17] Slow breathing can allow a person to cope with critical emotional and psychological events. In addition, a person can alter the type, rate, and ratio of breaths in order to engage the vagal pathways to send the right messages to the neural system.[18] One example is the "4-7-8" breathing technique, in which the person inhales for a count of 4, holds the breath for a count of 7, and slowly exhales for a count of 8. The key here is that the inhalation is half as long as the exhalation, which has been shown to have a calming effect during states of agitation or anxiety. Leaders are encouraged to use breathing techniques to strengthen the social engagement system during times of distress.

Eye and Body Movements

Eye contact and body movement have a strong impact on a person's perception of safety and danger cues. In *Polyvagal Exercises for Safety and Connection*, Deb Dana explains that stable facial expressions, eye gaze, and body movements often reflect signals of safety, whereas the absence of these signs is usually perceived as cues of danger. For that reason, leaders need to understand how their eye and body movements can be used to regulate their body's autonomic responses. Eye contact and body movements are evidence-based measures that can be integrated into the organizational setting to strengthen social engagement.

Orienting Attention

Trying to focus on several issues, tasks, and concerns at the same time can quickly result in overload. Orienting attention involves placing a sufficient level of attention on a certain goal, strategy, or something else of importance—in other words, concentrating on just that one thing. Different regulation strategies have different cognitive, affective, and social consequences.[19] In the case of orienting attention, research shows that it is aligned with perception and action, thereby explaining why changes in a person's attention have an effect on their behaviors and actions.[20] Concentration can mediate an individual's responses to surrounding stimuli, especially when dealing with stressful events. In essence, when leaders are paying close attention to something in the external environment, for instance, they are less likely to be consumed by anxious or agitated thoughts.

Vocalization

The human autonomic nervous system is particularly sensitive to sound, so it can allow people to exploit different neural pathways to strengthen cognitive functioning. The Polyvagal Theory highlights correlations between the striated muscles of the head and the production of sound through the pharyngeal muscles of the respiratory system.[21] As a result, vocalization exercises (such as singing, humming, and even laughing) not only help improve and regulate the autonomic state but also improve one's ability to communicate. Since autonomic regulation is entwined with listening, auditory processes, and vocalization,[22] it works both ways. Leaders are encouraged to engage in vocalization exercises as well as to speak in a soothing way to create a calming effect in the organizational setting. A lighter tone of voice is interpreted by the brain as more friendly, whereas loud, deeper tones may be received as hostile or aggressive.

Grounding Meditation

Meditation has become a popular method to help people control their mental, emotional, and psychological responses. In this context, we're speaking specifically about meditation strategies that are aligned with the autonomic nervous system, or grounding meditation. This can involve simply sitting and noticing where the body feels connection with the chair or the floor, tracking the breath, or observing any sounds in the environment, all while striving to imagine taking one's awareness and dropping out of the head (like taking an elevator down), and focusing on awareness of bodily sensations—trying to separate from conscious thought. It's similar to mindfulness meditation training in this way. In *The Polyvagal Theory in Therapy: Engaging the Rhythm of Regulation*, Deb Dana shares the "Autonomic Navigation Meditation," which encourages participants to anchor themselves to the ventral vagal state and to safely connect to sympathetic and dorsal vagal pathways. She writes, "'Plant your flag' in the territory of your ventral vagal state. Feel yourself rooted in the energy of safety this system offers. Your breath is full. Each exhalation moves you along the pathway that supports safety and connection. There is a rhythm to your heart rate. The beat brings well-being."[23] This is just a small sampling of her insightful work, and we encourage you to delve deeper into this.

●   ●   ●

Some of these skills and techniques can be used in the moment during an intense situation—for example, breathing to regulate the autonomic nervous system by slowing the breath, or counting while inhaling, holding, and exhaling, or orienting one's attention on the most pressing task in the face of work overload. Meanwhile, some nonconventional regulation skills, such as yoga and martial arts, which have not been discussed here, can be practiced in groups and individually. In all cases, continued practice of any combination of regulation skills can strengthen the body's ability to return to a state of calm more quickly in stressful situations.

Working Successfully with Others

Conflict is an inevitable problem in any personal or professional relationship. So, in addition to nurturing intuition and regulating the autonomic nervous system, an instinctive leader needs to understand how to deal with challenging scenarios without escalating them. During conflicts, it is common for an individual's autonomic state to be overridden by the mobilization or immobilization state. For that reason, leaders need to develop an instinctive understanding of effective socialization strategies that can mitigate the transition to the defense states. We'll offer some relatable examples to illustrate how to deal with two all-too-common issues: a supervisor who micromanages employees and an irate customer. These examples can be applied to any heated interaction in the workplace.

Dealing with a Micromanaging Supervisor

As if Oliver Green hasn't had enough challenges in his role as the youngest senior executive at a stock trading company, his greatest challenge has been his direct supervisor, Mr. Stone. Stone is known for being a strict boss. He often uses aggressive methods to ensure that his employees follow his rules. Furthermore, he always punishes employees who do not comply with his rules to set an example for others. From Stone's perspective, Oliver did not deserve the promotion because he lacks enough professional experience and the right instincts. For that reason, he has been keeping a close watch on Oliver's performance, looking for instances where Oliver underperforms or makes mistakes. This management style has become a major cause of concern for Oliver, who feels like his performance and decision-making are declining in this intimidating environment. In comparison, Stone does not like Oliver's leadership style nor his organizational choices. The two frequently engage in heated exchanges that make the work environment more hostile to other workers. To be effective and productive, Oliver needs to learn how to interact with supervisors who are easily mobilized.

In this case, Oliver's main challenge involves Stone's predisposition toward the mobilization state. As a person who has dealt with many conflicts, Stone relies on strict leadership styles that limit the freedom of his subordinates. Oliver's aggressive responses escalate the issue by pushing Stone further into the mobilization state. This rationale explains the heated arguments between the colleagues.

The first step in controlling the issue requires Oliver to regulate his autonomic response through appropriate methods. Many of these can be performed discreetly and quickly. For example, Oliver can simply adjust the rate of his breathing. After calming down, Oliver should provide cues of safety (such as a relaxed facial expression) to Stone to activate his social engagement system. Consequently, Oliver needs to use a friendly and inviting tone to stimulate socialization and allow the supervisor to be more receptive to proposed recommendations or ideas. These cues of safety are more useful for bargaining and increasing acceptance of unique ideas than cues of danger. In the end, the two employees will reestablish true cooperative communication and improve constructive prosocial behaviors with each other.

Dealing with an Irate Customer

One of Oliver's most difficult challenges involves interacting with dissatisfied customers. He has seen many instances in which customers have lost money due to their own poor investment choices, usually resulting in understandable disappointment but sometimes even rage. During one such instance, longtime client Ms. Russet came to Oliver's office to report that she'd lost several thousand dollars in just a few weeks. She was furious, and all attempts Oliver made to calm her down were futile. Not only was she rude but also extremely abusive. After being insulted for several minutes, Oliver aggressively criticized each of Russet's unwise investment choices. The interaction quickly turned heated, and Ms. Russet had to be forcefully escorted out of the building by security. "I'm taking my money elsewhere!" she exclaimed just before the door closed behind her.

Mr. Stone, Oliver's direct supervisor, and the other senior managers raised concerns regarding Oliver's response to the situation. They feared that if Oliver was permitted to handle customer complaints in the future, the company would lose more clients. How might Oliver have avoided the escalation of this conflict?

You are probably familiar with how people who are around anxious or agitated people seem to get irritable or angry themselves. Oliver's case illustrates how one person in an elevated sympathetic state fosters a similar response in others around them: Ms. Russet's verbal attack caused Oliver to descend the ladder himself, because he wasn't yet equipped with the right tools to regulate his state.

What's more, the conflict between Oliver and the customer involves an ancient dilemma: "Is the customer always right?" While some organizations prioritize their customers and view them as the most critical stakeholders, others place more emphasis on their employees. In this context, the most effective resolution requires organizations to view customers and employees as equal stakeholders.

The first step in addressing conflict with a customer is for the employee to regulate their autonomic state in a manner that strengthens the ventral vagal pathways to support socialization. If Oliver had done this using the regulation skills he's diligently practicing these days, he would have been more resilient against the customer's complaints and insults. Then, once Oliver had regulated, he could have guided the customer by using cues of safety (positive body language, eye contact, and facial expressions) to make her more receptive to mutual cooperation—without being condescending. Oliver also needed to acknowledge Ms. Russet's feelings by showing sympathy in a friendly and nonintimidating manner. This approach would give the two parties the opportunity to listen to each other instead of encouraging them to escalate the conflict.

When dealing with an agitated customer or coworker who is in a sympathetic state, the best approach is to somewhat match the higher energy level but with a more friendly, social tone. If Oliver had appeared too calm or sedate, for instance, it would only serve to increase his customer's agitation. You know how it goes: if someone casually tells an upset person to "calm down," it's likely the exact opposite of what they end up doing! So, if a customer or coworker is in the mobilization state, trying to match their energy level while slowing down and softening the voice just enough can help the leader connect with them more effectively. This approach would help Oliver interact with customers as equal stakeholders of the organization—and Mr. Stone would have one less thing to complain about regarding Oliver's performance.

Setting Up the Physical Environment to Provide Cues of Safety

Research reveals several passive methods for controlling engagement in the organizational setting to produce positive results. The active method involves conscious and voluntary behaviors that aim to support social engagement by regulating the autonomic state, but leaders can also passively regulate their staff's defense state by making adjustments to the environment.[24] While the active method to bring about feelings of safety is achieved by exercising appropriate neural resources, passive methods aim to induce feelings of safety using external sources.[25] We'll discuss these passive methods now with a focus on how leaders and organizations can positively influence their workers' autonomic states through colors, lighting, furniture, plants, view, and sound. Again, this is not a comprehensive overview, so we encourage you to delve more deeply into this topic, knowing that your efforts will be worthwhile.

Colors

Considerable research has been performed to investigate how colors influence employee productivity. Researchers performed a review of 40 papers revealing that color has a significant impact on human perception and behavior. They concluded that certain colors, such as bright and warm colors, can create an appealing environment that encourages workers to deliver optimal performance. Colors that are usually perceived to have a positive influence on mood are blue and green, though blue was also shown to have a drowsy and sleep effect. In addition, some colors have a greater effect on physiological processes, such as heart rate. For example, a red room has shown to put the brain into a more excited state.[26] These findings explain the importance of color in the workplace with regard to creating an environment that has positive effects on employees' autonomic states and, as a result, on their decision-making. Clearly, there are many nuances to color choice that should be taken into consideration when designing or redesigning the work environment.

Lighting

Workplace lighting can play an equally important role as interior design. Reliable research explains that exposure to certain types of light can improve biological processes, mood, and alertness.[27] Alertness is both a behavioral and a physiological state of responsiveness to internal and external stimuli. For instance, cool-white light can improve employee awareness while also reducing eye irritation and discomfort. Furthermore, altering the balance of direct and indirect light can allow the organization to communicate a certain message. For example, more direct, bright lighting conveys energy and excitement, whereas softer lighting is more soothing and promotes a sense of calm. The lighting can also be adjusted based on the time of the day. For example, exposure to morning or afternoon light can alleviate depression among workers.[28] This rationale explains why light has become a popular tool for addressing mental health issues. Bright light therapy is based on the assumption that exposure to certain levels of light can mitigate psychological and physical barriers.[29] Mental health issues aside, lighting can have a significant impact on the workers' state. Overall, organizations need to research what type of lighting will improve employee productivity and wellness in the workplace.

Furniture

Furniture is another vital component of the organizational environment that can influence employee mood and performance. Office furniture should be set up in a manner that enhances the freedom and openness of the workers. Research shows that the characteristics of the furniture and interior space can either be a source of environmental stress or a tool for relaxation and social cohesion.[30] In other words, impractical furniture can hinder employees from delivering their full potential, whereas the introduction of practical furniture can increase employee satisfaction and engagement. Open pathways and spaces can strengthen social engagement and prevent workers from shifting to the mobilization or immobilization state. Overall, innovative and multifunctional furniture setups can improve office communication and employee wellness.

Plants

Indoor and outdoor plants can play a similar role as colors and interior design in terms of regulating employees' autonomic responses. Research shows that most people spend the majority of their daily lives indoors. As a result, prolonged interactions with enclosed environments and information technology can become a cause of distress among workers. To address this problem, organizations need to create a natural indoor environment that positively stimulates the workers' autonomic responses.[31] Healthy, thriving plants can create a warm and safe environment for workers that encourages them to remain in the socialization state.

View

Another approach for creating a conducive workplace involves the manipulation of the surrounding view. The ideal office workspace is laid out in a manner that properly portrays the aesthetic beauty of the surroundings. With the rapid advancement of real estate and interior design, various new designs have been established that allow workers to appreciate a natural or artificial view.

The natural view may consist of vegetation and wildlife, whereas the artificial view may highlight surrounding architecture and infrastructure. These settings can be established depending on the office layout and the organization's work culture.

Sound

Ambient sound or music can appeal to workers' social engagement state. In most cases, noise is usually associated with adverse effects on employee performance and productivity, depending on the type of noise.[32] However, the use of ambient music or mild background noise (white, brown, or pink) can provide a soothing auditory stimulus to workers. (White noise contains all frequencies, while brown and pink noise emphasize lower frequencies and a more bass sound. Brown noise has the most bass, and some consider it the most soothing. It can be compared to the sound you hear riding in an airplane at night.)[33] Such sounds can help workers to deliver their full potential. Still, leaders need to ensure that the sound has appropriate magnitudes to prevent it from distracting the workers from their respective roles.

KEY POINTS

- Instinctive intelligence is an integral skill that modern leaders need to nurture to cultivate a productive work environment and a satisfied staff.
- With the rising complexity of organizational processes, leaders face more challenges that can easily push them from socialization to mobilization and immobilization states.
- When leaders identify the root causes of their autonomic responses and nurture instinctive intelligence, they are more capable of maintaining an optimal autonomic state.
- Exercising the vagal brake, practicing other regulation skills, and using autonomic maps can be integrated into both social and hostile work environments.
- A conducive work environment that exudes warmth and safety can engage the active and passive pathways of workers' autonomic nervous system.

CONCLUSION

Throughout this book, senior executive Oliver Green has not only experienced myriad challenges but also opportunities to improve his efficacy as an instinctive leader and enjoy the positive outcomes. He understands that he needs to bridge the experience gap separating him from his more senior colleagues so that he can learn to rely more on instinct when the situation calls for it. To develop confidence in his gut instinct and balance it with his analytical talents, he is motivated to develop a deeper understanding of himself and his team members. He is also aware that it is beneficial to seek support when necessary.

Oliver has tried various leadership approaches, settling upon one that works for him and his team, and has learned to connect with his employees on a base level. He has also learned to use intrinsic and extrinsic drivers to improve his department's motivation and overall productivity. He knows how to access his vagal brake and use safety cues with the people he interacts with—including disgruntled clients and his direct supervisor. Overall, he is more confident when making financial and organizational decisions. He has developed a good understanding of his potential biases both in the recruitment process and in financial decision-making and knows that, during times of distress, he may fall back on these. He takes steps now to return to a more stable foundation from which to make these important decisions.

After all the ups and downs, Oliver understands that being an instinctive leader requires a combination of rational and nonrational mental faculties, as well as deciding when to use a dual cognitive approach or just one. Oliver's ongoing objective is to balance rational and nonrational thinking to create a steadfast foundation from which to operate his department and perform his duties. He acknowledges that instinctive leadership requires a combination of unique strengths and strategies to capitalize fully on the available opportunities. Oliver has come a long way.

Throughout this book, we've discussed the most effective mechanisms for promoting rational and nonrational decision-making. We've relied on the Polyvagal Theory to explain how human behavior is affected by changes in the autonomic nervous system. We've then taken this discussion beyond the physiologic processes behind the Polyvagal Theory to focus on its applications in organizational decision-making. While various leadership strategies rely on either rational or nonrational psychological considerations, instinctive leadership requires a leader to determine when to rely on an intuitive approach, when to use an integrated approach of both intuitive and rational decision-making, and when to fully analyze a situation prior to making a decision. Despite the disparity between rational and nonrational decision-making, these two faculties play equally vital roles in terms of guiding decision-making.

Instinctive leaders intuitively understand how to manage staff and delegate responsibilities and have a comprehensive understanding of teamwork. Such leaders are able to maneuver between the three autonomic states without negatively affecting the organization's performance. Most teams experience conflicts due to communication issues or poor work environments, resulting in simple mistakes that can easily escalate into serious organizational problems. Thus, the instinctive leader is obligated to embody the key characteristics and traits that define leadership, turning to the best strategies for constructing resilient teams, including conflict-resolution training.

Instinctive leaders also understand that even the best human resource management approaches can end in futility. Despite the leader's efforts, some employees may still show low job satisfaction and motivation levels. This is when the instinctive leader evaluates whether the worker's motivation is derived from their intrinsic or extrinsic needs and puts strategies in place to help meet their specific needs. Since a mismatch between the worker's baseline autonomic state and their job characteristics may also be the cause of employee dissatisfaction, the instinctive leader makes necessary organizational changes to ensure that an employee's baseline state reflects their job requirements and demands. An instinctive leader further ensures that employees spend their time at work most often in the vagal parasympathetic state by taking steps such as frequently using cues of safety and ensuring that the interior design of the work environment promotes feelings of safety.

With regard to talent acquisition, an instinctive leader is aware of a range of factors that influence the process. In cases of stress, trauma, and anxiety, the likelihood of bias and discrimination can increase drastically. The negative factors can be mitigated by taking steps to return to a socialization state where biases can be recognized for what they are and avoided.

In the real-life business environment, decisions are determined by an individual's perceptions of their surroundings. For instance, the evaluation of financial risks and rewards depends on whether the worker relies on objective or subjective viewpoints. The cultivation of instinctive leadership can fail if the leader lacks a coherent understanding of their personal identity and perspective. This rationale is based on the principles of neuroception and interoception, which encourage the brain to make decisions based on both the surrounding and internal physiologic environments. Once individuals have this understanding, they can nurture instinctive leadership in several ways: (1) maintain an optimal autonomic state (the socialization state is considered the optimal state because it supports maximum decision-making), (2) manipulate the autonomic state as needed using regulation skills, and (3) cultivate and learn to rely on intuitive intelligence to make rapid decisions with minimal adverse outcomes.

It is our sincere hope that this book has enlightened current and future leaders on the benefits of applying the Polyvagal Theory to better implement instinctive decision-making and remain steadfast in the face of myriad work-related challenges each day. The science-based theories, strategies, and findings discussed throughout this book can be used by any leader, including young leaders like Oliver Green, future leaders who have not yet unlocked the potential of their rational and nonrational mental faculties, and more seasoned leaders who are struggling to enhance productivity and the well-being of their staff. The concepts and theories highlighted in this book will guide future generations in the cultivation of instinctive leadership.

ACKNOWLEDGMENTS

Understanding human behavior and what motivates us has always been a core principle in the fields of psychology and psychiatry. Randy would like to first and foremost express gratitude to his friend and coauthor, Geoffrey VanderPal, for his time, interest, and thoughtful exploration of how neuroscience informs existing gaps in leadership, management, and behavioral finance.

None of our early exploratory work would be possible without the discovery of Polyvagal Theory by Stephen Porges, a brilliant scientist who helped us understand how the human fascination with complex cognitive models led to essentially abandoning an understanding of our whole nervous system.

Critically, it was the efforts and skills of Deborah Dana, a gifted mental health professional, who translated the theory into clinical practice. Deb and her work have been an inspiration and source of support in our journey, and she has kindly reviewed our work and written the Foreword.

Randy would also like to thank Abi Blakeslee, SEP, CMT, MFT, PhD, who has been a dear friend and a mentor. Her teaching and support, as well as her warmth and kindness, have been critical in his development as a professional.

Additionally, Larry Villano, CEO of Resilient Health, a local nonprofit in Arizona, was the first business leader to foster Randy's interest in exploring these concepts but was an enthusiastic supporter who led the integration of Polyvagal Theory into his organization.

Finally, we would like to thank Randall Redfield, executive director at the Polyvagal Institute, for his support in developing this project. His leadership has been critical in bringing this important theory to a wider audience.

NOTES

CHAPTER 1

1. Porges, Stephen W., "The Polyvagal Theory: New Insights into Adaptive Reactions of the Autonomic Nervous System," *Cleveland Clinic Journal of Medicine* 76, Suppl 2 (April 2009): S86–S90, doi:10.3949/ccjm.76.s2.17,https://www.ncbi.nlm.nih.gov/pmc/articles/PMC3108032/.

2. Porges, "The Polyvagal Theory: New Insights into Adaptive Reactions."

3. Sullivan, M.B., et al., "Yoga Therapy and Polyvagal Theory: The Convergence of Traditional Wisdom and Contemporary Neuroscience for Self-Regulation and Resilience," *Frontiers in Human Neuroscience* 12 (2018): 67.

4. Sullivan et al., "Yoga Therapy and Polyvagal Theory," 67.

5. Sullivan et al., "Yoga Therapy and Polyvagal Theory," 67.

6. Kolacz, J., K. K. Kovacic, and S. W. Porges, "Traumatic Stress and the Autonomic Brain-Gut Connection in Development: Polyvagal Theory as an Integrative Framework for Psychosocial and Gastrointestinal Pathology," *Developmental Psychobiology* 61, no. 5 (2019): 3, https://doi.org/10.1002/dev.21852.

7. Juhro, Solikin M., and A. Farid Aulia, "Transformational Leadership Through Applied Neuroscience: Transmission Mechanism of the Thinking Process," *BI Institute Working Paper* 7, no. 3 (July 2017): 1–22, https://ijol.cikd.ca/article_60394.html.

8. Calabretta, G., G. Gemser, and N. M. Wijnberg, "The Interplay Between Intuition and Rationality in Strategic Decision Making: A Paradox Perspective," *Organization Studies* 38, no. 3–4 (2016): 365–401.

9. Calabretta, Gemser, and Wijnberg, "Interplay Between Intuition," 365–401.

10. Gigerenzer, G., and W. Gaissmaier, (2015), "Decision Making: Nonrational Theories," *International Encyclopedia of the Social & Behavioral Sciences* (2015): 911–916.
11. Porges, S. W., "Polyvagal Theory: A Biobehavioral Journey to Sociality," *Comprehensive Psychoneuroendocrinology* 7 (2021), 100069.
12. Porges, "Polyvagal Theory: A Biobehavioral Journey to Sociality."
13. Porges, "Polyvagal Theory: A Biobehavioral Journey to Sociality."
14. Andreassi, J. L., *Psychophysiology: Human Behavior and Physiological Response*, 5th ed. (Mahwah, NJ: Psychology Press, 2006), cited in De Looff et al., "Aggressive Behaviour, Burnout and Physiology," *Expertisecentrum de Borg*, 2019.
15. Dana, Deb, *Polyvagal Exercises for Safety and Connection: 50 Client-Centered Practices* (New York: W. W. Norton & Company, 2020), 33.
16. Dana, *Polyvagal Exercises*, 31.
17. Beauchaine, T. P., L. Gatzke-Kopp, and H. K. Mead, "Polyvagal Theory and Developmental Psychopathology: Emotion Dysregulation and Conduct Problems from Preschool to Adolescence," *Biological Psychology* 74, no. 2 (2007): 174–184, https://www.ncbi.nlm.nih.gov/pmc/articles/PMC1801075/.
18. Beauchaine, Gatzke-Kopp, and Mead, "Polyvagal Theory," 174–184.
19. Porges, S. W., "Cardiac Vagal Tone: A Neurophysiological Mechanism That Evolved in Mammals to Dampen Threat Reactions and Promote Sociality," *World Psychiatry* 20, no. 2 (2021): 296.
20. Kolacz, J., K. K. Kovacic, and S. W. Porges, "Traumatic Stress and the Autonomic Brain-Gut Connection in Development: Polyvagal Theory as an Integrative Framework for Psychosocial and Gastrointestinal Pathology," *Developmental Psychobiology* 61, no. 5 (2019): 3, https://doi.org/10.1002/dev.21852.
21. Ernsberger, U., T. Deller, and H. Rohrer, "The Sympathies of the Body: Functional Organization and Neuronal Differentiation in the Peripheral Sympathetic Nervous System," *Cell and Tissue Research* 386, no. 3 (2021): 455–475.
22. Kolacz, Kovacic, and Porges, "Traumatic Stress and the Autonomic Brain-Gut Connection," 3.
23. Dana, *The Polyvagal Theory in Therapy: Engaging the Rhythm of Regulation* (New York: W. W. Norton & Company, 2018), 19.
24. Dana, *The Polyvagal Theory in Therapy*, 19.
25. Dana, *The Polyvagal Theory in Therapy*, 19.
26. Dana, *The Polyvagal Theory in Therapy*, 20.

27. Porges, S. W., "The Polyvagal Perspective," *Biological Psychology* 74, no. 2 (2007): 116–143.

28. Soosalu, G., S. Henwood, and A. Deo, "Head, Heart, and Gut in Decision Making: Development of a Multiple Brain Preference Questionnaire," *Sage Open* 9, no. 1 (2019): https://doi.org/10.1177/2158244019837439.

29. Soosalu, Henwood, and Deo, "Head, Heart, and Gut."

30. Goler, L., J. Gale, B. Harrington, and A. Grant, "Why People Really Quit their Jobs," *Harvard Business Review*, January 11, 2018, https://hbr.org/2018/01/why-people-really-quit-their-jobs.

31. Gallup, *State of the Global Workplace: 2022 Report*, https://www.gallup.com/workplace/349484/state-of-the-global-workplace-2022-report.aspx.

32. Santomauro, D. F., et al., "Global Prevalence and Burden of Depressive and Anxiety Disorders in 204 Countries and Territories in 2020 Due to the COVID-19 Pandemic," *The Lancet* 398, no. 10312(2021): 1700–1712.

33. Elliott, D., "World Mental Health Day: 5 Powerful Quotes on Mental Health," *The World Economic Forum*, October 9, 2020, https://www.weforum.org/agenda/2020/10/mental-health-quotes-prince-william-obama-ardern/.

CHAPTER 2

1. Hunt, T., and L. Fedynich, "Leadership: Past, Present, and Future: An Evolution of an Idea," *Journal of Arts and Humanities* 8, no. 2 (2019): 22–26.

2. Hunt and Fedynich, "Leadership."

3. Frederickson, J. J., I. Messina, and A. Grecucci, "Dysregulated Anxiety and Dysregulating Defenses: Toward an Emotion Regulation Informed Dynamic Psychotherapy," *Frontiers in Psychology* 2054 (2018), doi.org/10.3389/fpsyg.2018.02054.

4. Calabretta, G., G. Gemser, and N. M. Wijnberg, "The Interplay Between Intuition and Rationality in Strategic Decision Making: A Paradox Perspective," *Organization Studies* 38, no. 3–4 (2016): 365–401.

5. Lucas, M. G., and S. Caspers, "Leadership and Adult Development: Towards a Unified Neuro-psycho-economic Approach," *Behavioral Development Bulletin* 19, no. 4 (2014): 83.

6. Vasconcelos, A. F., "Intuition, Prayer, and Managerial Decision-Making Processes: A Religion-Based Framework," *Management Decision* 47, no. 6 (2009): 930–949.

7. Vasconcelos, "Intuition, Prayer, and Managerial Decision-Making Processes," 932.
8. Potter, D., and J. Starke, *Building a Culture of Conscious Leadership* (Boca Raton, FL: Taylor and Francis, 2022).
9. Aga, D. A., "Transactional Leadership and Project Success: The Moderating Role of Goal Clarity," *Procedia Computer Science* 100 (2016): 517–525.
10. Aga, "Transactional Leadership and Project Success."
11. Potter, D., and J. Starke, *Building a Culture of Conscious Leadership* (Boca Raton, FL: Taylor and Francis, 2022).
12. Potter and Starke, *Building a Culture of Conscious Leadership.*
13. Xenikou, A., "Transformational Leadership, Transactional Contingent Reward, and Organizational Identification: The Mediating Effect of Perceived Innovation and Goal Culture Orientations," *Frontiers in Psychology* 8 (2017): 1754.
14. Potter and Starke, *Building a Culture of Conscious Leadership.*
15. Xenikou, "Transformational Leadership, Transactional Contingent Reward, and Organizational Identification," 1754.
16. Hoxha, A., "Transformational and Transactional Leadership Styles on Employee Performance," *International Journal of Humanities and Social Science Invention* (2019): 2319–7722.
17. Potter and Starke, *Building a Culture of Conscious Leadership.*
18. Jensen, U. T., et al., "Conceptualizing and Measuring Transformational and Transactional Leadership," *Administration and Society* 51, no. 1 (2016): 3–33.
19. Specchia, M. L., et al., "Leadership Styles and Nurses' Job Satisfaction: Results of a Systematic Review," *International Journal of Environmental Research and Public Health* 18, no. 4 (2021): 1552.
20. Odumeru, J. A., and I. G. Ogbonna, "Transformational vs. Transactional Leadership Theories: Evidence in Literature," *International Review of Management and Business Research* 2, no. 2 (2013): 355.
21. Potter and Starke, *Building a Culture of Conscious Leadership.*
22. Khan, H., et al., "Impact of Transformational Leadership on Work Performance, Burnout and Social Loafing: A Mediation Model," *Future Business Journal* 6, no. 1 (2020): 1–13.
23. Jensen, U. T., and L. L. Bro, "How Transformational Leadership Supports Intrinsic Motivation and Public Service Motivation: The Mediating Role of Basic Need Satisfaction," *The American Review of Public Administration* 48, no. 6 (2017): 535–549.
24. Choi, S. L., et al., "Transformational Leadership, Empowerment, and Job Satisfaction: The Mediating Role of Employee Empowerment," *Human Resources for Health* 14, no. 1 (2016): 1–14.

25. Khalili, A., "Linking Transformational Leadership, Creativity, Innovation, and Innovation-Supportive Climate," *Management Decision* 54, no. 9 (2016): 2277–2293.

26. Tepper, B. J., et al., "Examining Follower Responses to Transformational Leadership from a Dynamic, Person–Environment Fit Perspective," *Academy of Management Journal* 61, no. 4 (2014): 1343–1368.

27. Khan et al., "Impact of Transformational Leadership on Work Performance, Burnout and Social Loafing."

28. Lai, F. Y., et al., "Transformational Leadership and Job Performance: The Mediating Role of Work Engagement," *SAGE Open* 10, no. 1 (2020).

29. Dong, Y., et al., "Enhancing Employee Creativity via Individual Skill Development and Team Knowledge Sharing: Influences of Dual-Focused Transformational Leadership," *Journal of Organizational Behavior* 38, no. 3 (2016): 439–458.

30. Jensen, U. T., et al., "Conceptualizing and Measuring Transformational and Transactional Leadership," *Administration and Society* 51, no. 1 (2016): 3–33.

31. Banks, G. C., et al., "A Meta-Analytic Review of Authentic and Transformational Leadership: A Test for Redundancy," *The Leadership Quarterly* 27, no. 4 (2016): 634–652.

32. Winston, B., and D. Fields, "Seeking and Measuring the Essential Behaviors of Servant Leadership," *Leadership & Organization Development Journal* 36, no. 4 (2015).

33. Winston and Fields, "Essential Behaviors of Servant Leadership."

34. Edmonds, S. C., *The Culture Engine: A Framework for Driving Results, Inspiring Your Employees, and Transforming Your Workplace* (New York: John Wiley & Sons, 2014).

35. Whittington, J. L., "Creating a Positive Organization Through Servant Leadership," in *Servant Leadership and Followership: Examining the Impact on Workplace Behavior*, ed. C. J. Davis (New York: Springer, 2017), 51–80.

36. Parris, D. L., and J. W. Peachey, "A Systematic Literature Review of Servant Leadership Theory in Organizational Contexts," *Journal of Business Ethics* 113, no. 3 (2013): 377–393.

37. Specchia, M. L., et al., "Leadership Styles and Nurses' Job Satisfaction: Results of a Systematic Review," *International Journal of Environmental Research and Public Health* 18, no. 4 (2021): 1552.

38. Winston and Fields, "Essential Behaviors of Servant Leadership."

39. Winston and Fields, "Essential Behaviors of Servant Leadership."

40. Ghazzawi, K., R. E. Shoughari, and B. E. Osta, "Situational Leadership and Its Effectiveness in Rising Employee Productivity: A Study on North Lebanon Organization," *Human Resource Management Research* 7, no. 3 (2017): 102–110.

41. Thompson, G., and L. Glasø, "Situational Leadership Theory: A Test from a Leader-Follower Congruence Approach," *Leadership & Organization Development Journal* 39, no. 5 (2018): 574–591.

42. Ghazzawi et al., "Situational Leadership and Its Effectiveness in Rising Employee Productivity."

43. Lynch, B., "Partnering for Performance in Situational Leadership: A Person-Centred Leadership Approach," *International Practice Development Journal* 5 (2015).

44. Wuryani, E., A. Rodlib, S. Sutarsib, N. Dewib, and D. Arifb, "Analysis of Decision Support System on Situational Leadership Styles on Work Motivation and Employee Performance," *Management Science Letters* 11, no. 2 (2021): 365–372.

45. Thompson, G., and L. Glasø, "Situational Leadership Theory: A Test from a Leader-Follower Congruence Approach," *Leadership & Organization Development Journal* 39, no. 5 (2018): 574–591.

46. Thompson and Glasø, "Situational Leadership."

47. Thompson and Glasø, "Situational Leadership."

48. Soosalu, G., S. Henwood, and A. Deo, "Head, Heart, and Gut in Decision Making: Development of a Multiple Brain Preference Questionnaire," *Sage Open* 9, no. 1 (2019): 2158244019837439.

49. Yu, R., "Stress Potentiates Decision Biases: A Stress Induced Deliberation-to-Intuition (SIDI) Model," *Neurobiology of Stress* 3 (2016): 83–95.

50. Yao, Y.H., et al., "Leadership, Work Stress and Employee Behavior," *Chinese Management Studies* 8, no. 1 (2014).

51. Furtner, M. R., U. Baldegger, and J. F. Rauthmann, "Leading Yourself and Leading Others: Linking Self-Leadership to Transformational, Transactional, and Laissez-Faire Leadership," *European Journal of Work and Organizational Psychology* 22, no. 4 (2012): 436–449.

52. Adler, A.B., et al., "Behavioral Health Leadership: New Directions in Occupational Mental Health," *Current Psychiatry Reports* 16, no. 10 (2014): 1–7.

53. Adler, et al., "Behavioral Health Leadership," 1–7.

54. Cuevas-Rodríguez, G., L. R. Gomez-Mejia, and R. M. Wiseman, "Has Agency Theory Run Its Course? Making the Theory More

Flexible to Inform the Management of Reward Systems," *Corporate Governance: An International Review* 20, no. 6 (2012): 526–546.

55. Islam, Q., M. H. Juraybi, and Y. M. Alraythi, "Effectiveness of Situational Leadership Style in Managing Workplace Crisis," *Saudi Journal of Business and Management Studies,* 6, no. 9 (2021): 362–365.

56. Harms, P.D., et al., "Leadership and Stress: A Meta-Analytic Review," *The Leadership Quarterly* 28, no. 1(2016): 178–194.

57. Djourova, N. P., et al., "Self- Efficacy and Resilience: Mediating Mechanisms in the Relationship Between the Transformational Leadership Dimensions and Well-Being," *Journal of Leadership & Organizational Studies* 27, no. 3(2020): 256–270.

58. Rhodes, C. "Ethics, Alterity and the Rationality of Leadership Justice," *Human Relations* 65, no. 10 (2012): 1311–1331.

59. Rhodes, "Ethics."

60. Baldomir, J., and J. P. Hood, "Servant Leadership as a Framework for Organizational Change," *International Leadership Journal* 8, no. 1 (2016).

61. Hess, J. D., and A. C. Bacigalupo, "Enhancing Decisions and Decision-Making Processes Through the Application of Emotional Intelligence Skills," *Management Decision* 49, no. 5 (2011): 710–721.

62. Islam, Q., M. H. Juraybi, and Y. M. Alraythi, "Effectiveness of Situational Leadership Style in Managing Workplace Crisis," *Saudi Journal of Business and Management Studies,* 6, no. 9 (2021): 362–365.

63. Islam, Juraybi, and Alraythi, "Effectiveness of Situational Leadership," 362–365.

64. Pasaribu, S. B., et al., "The Role of Situational Leadership on Job Satisfaction, Organizational Citizenship Behavior (OCB), and Employee Performance," *Frontiers in Psychology* 13 (2022).

65. Ghazzawi et al., "Situational Leadership and Its Effectiveness in Rising Employee Productivity."

66. Balasubramanian, S., and C. Fernandes, "Confirmation of a Crisis Leadership Model and Its Effectiveness: Lessons from the COVID-19 Pandemic," *Cogent Business & Management* 9, no. 1 (2022): 2022824.

67. Balasubramanian and Fernandes, "Crisis Leadership Model," 2022824.

CHAPTER 3

1. Podsiadlowski, A., and C. Ward, "Global Mobility and Bias in the Workplace," *The Psychology of Global Mobility* (2010): 279–300.

2. VanderPal, G., and R. Brazie, "Exploratory Study of Polyvagal Theory and Underlying Stress and Trauma That Influence Major Leadership Approaches," *Journal of Applied Business and Economics* 24, no. 1 (2022).

3. O'Meara, B., and S. Petzall, *Handbook of Strategic Recruitment and Selection: A Systems Approach* (Bingley, UK: Emerald Group Publishing, 2013).

4. Clarke, J. A., "Explicit Bias," *Northwestern University Law Review* 113 (2018): 505.

5. Whysall, Z., "Cognitive Biases in Recruitment, Selection, and Promotion: The Risk of Subconscious Discrimination," in *Hidden Inequalities in the Workplace: A Guide to the Current Challenges, Issues and Business Solutions* (Palgrave MacMillan, 2018), 215–243.

6. Maurer, R., "Recruiters' Stress Significantly Increased in 2020," SHRM, November 18, 2020, https://www.shrm.org /resourcesandtools/hr-topics/talent-acquisition/pages/recruiters-stress-significantly-increased-2020.aspx.

7. Winter, L., "Organizational Trauma: A Phenomenological Study of Psychological Organizational Trauma and Its Effect on Employees and Organization," *Management* (18544223) 14, no. 2 (2019).

8. Kozlowska, K., et al., "Fear and the Defense Cascade: Clinical Implications and Management," *Harvard Review of Psychiatry* 23, no. 4 (July/August 2015): 263–287, doi:10.1097/HRP .0000000000000065.

9. Potočnik, K., et al., "Paving the Way for Research in Recruitment and Selection: Recent Developments, Challenges and Future Opportunities," *European Journal of Work and Organizational Psychology* 30, no. 2 (2021): 159–174.

10. Sawyer, P. J., et al., "Discrimination and the Stress Response: Psychological and Physiological Consequences of Anticipating Prejudice in Interethnic Interactions," *American Journal of Public Health* 102, no. 5 (2012): 1020–1026.

11. Dana, Deb, *Polyvagal Exercises for Safety and Connection: 50 Client-Centered Practices* (New York: W. W. Norton & Company, 2020).

12. Dana, *Polyvagal Exercises.*

13. Sullivan, M. B., et al., "Yoga Therapy and Polyvagal Theory: The Convergence of Traditional Wisdom and Contemporary

Neuroscience for Self-Regulation and Resilience," *Frontiers in Human Neuroscience* 12 (2018): 67.

14. VanderPal, G., and R. Brazie, "Influence of Basic Human Behaviors (Influenced by Brain Architecture and Function), and Past Traumatic Events on Investor Behavior and Financial Bias," *Journal of Accounting and Finance* 22, no. 2 (2022): 14.

15. Seijts, G. H., and J. Gandz, "Transformational Change and Leader Character," *Business Horizons* 61, no. 2 (2017): 239–249.

16. VanderPal and Brazie, "Exploratory Study of Polyvagal Theory."

17. Al-Hawari, M. A., S. Bani-Melhem, and S. Quratulain, "Do Frontline Employees Cope Effectively with Abusive Supervision and Customer Incivility? Testing the Effect of Employee Resilience," *Journal of Business and Psychology* 35 (2019): 223–240.

18. Al-Hawari, Bani-Melhem, and Quratulain, "Do Frontline Employees Cope Effectively."

19. Sullivan et al., "Yoga Therapy and Polyvagal Theory."

20. Kearney, T., et al., "Emotional Intelligence in Front-Line/Back-Office Employee Relationships," *Journal of Services Marketing* 31, no. 2, (2017): 185–199.

21. Livermore, J. J., et al., "Approach-Avoidance Decisions Under Threat: The Role of Autonomic Psychophysiological States," *Frontiers in Neuroscience* 15 (2021): 621517.

22. Kearney, et al., "Emotional Intelligence."

23. Berry, D., and M. P. Bell, "Inequality in Organizations: Stereotyping, Discrimination, and Labor Law Exclusions," *Equality, Diversity and Inclusion: An International Journal* 31, no. 3 (2012): 236–248.

24. Stamarski, C. S., and L. S. Son-Hing, "Gender Inequalities in the Workplace: The Effects of Organizational Structures, Processes, Practices, and Decision Makers' Sexism," *Frontiers in Psychology* 6 (2015): 1400.

25. McFadden, C., "Lesbian, Gay, Bisexual, and Transgender Careers and Human Resource Development: A Systematic Literature Review," *Human Resource Development Review* 14.2 (2015): 125–162.

26. VanderPal and Brazie, "Influence of Basic Human Behaviors."

27. Smith, S., et al., "A Multi-institutional Exploration of the Social Mobility Potential of Degree Apprenticeships," *Journal of Education and Work* 34, no. 4 (2021): 488–503.

28. Malinen, S., and L. Johnston, "Workplace Ageism: Discovering Hidden Bias," *Experimental Aging Research* 39, no. 4 (2013): 445–465.

29. Lindsay, S., "Discrimination and Other Barriers to Employment for Teens and Young Adults with Disabilities," *Disability and Rehabilitation* 33, nos. 15–16 (2011): 1340–1350.

30. Swartz, T. H., et al., "The Science and Value of Diversity: Closing the Gaps in Our Understanding of Inclusion and Diversity," *The Journal of Infectious Diseases* 220, Supplement 2 (2019): S33–S41.

31. Derous, E., and A. M. Ryan, "When Your Resume Is (Not) Turning You Down: Modelling Ethnic Bias in Resume Screening," *Human Resource Management Journal* 29, no. 2 (2019): 113–130.

32. Albert, E. T., "AI in Talent Acquisition: A Review of AI Applications Used in Recruitment and Selection," *Strategic HR Review* 18, no.5 (2019): 215–221.

33. Maurer, R., "Recruiters' Stress Significantly Increased in 2020," SHRM, November 18, 2020, https://www.shrm.org/resourcesandtools/hr-topics/talent-acquisition/pages/recruiters-stress-significantly-increased-2020.aspx.

34. VanderPal and Brazie, "Influence of Basic Human Behaviors."

35. Landsbergis, P. A. "Interventions to Reduce Job Stress and Improve Work Organization and Worker Health," *Unhealthy Work* (Routledge, 2018), 193–209.

36. Porges, S. W., and D. Dana, *Clinical Applications of the Polyvagal Theory: The Emergence of Polyvagal-Informed Therapies* (New York: W. W. Norton & Company, 2018), 62.

37. Porges and Dana, *Clinical Applications of Polyvagal Theory*, 62.

38. Brooks, S., G. J. Rubin, and N. Greenberg, "Managing Traumatic Stress in the Workplace," *Occupational Medicine* 69, no. 1 (2019): 2–4.

39. Porges and Dana, *Clinical Applications of the Polyvagal Theory*, 62.

CHAPTER 4

1. Calomiris, C. W., and L. Neal, "History of Financial Globalization, Overview," in *Handbook of Key Global Financial Markets, Institutions and Infrastructure* (Cambridge, Mass.: Academic Press 2012), 3–14.

2. Frydman, C., and C. F. Camerer, "The Psychology and Neuroscience of Financial Decision Making," *Trends in Cognitive Sciences* 20, no. 9 (2016): 661–675.

3. Frydman and Camerer, "Psychology and Neuroscience."

4. Park, M., "Objective vs Subjective Trading," Corporate Finance Institute, updated February 23, 2023, https://corporatefinanceinstitute.com/resources/capital-markets/objective-vs-subjective-trading/.
5. Park, "Objective vs Subjective Trading."
6. Crabtree, J., "Gut Instinct: Do Traders Have a Sixth Sense?," CNBC, September 20, 2016, https://www.cnbc.com/2016/09/20/gut-instinct-do-traders-have-a-sixth-sense.html.
7. University of Cambridge, "'Gut Feelings' Help Make More Successful Financial Traders," University of Cambridge, September 19, 2016, https://www.cam.ac.uk/research/news/gut-feelings-help-make-more-successful-financial-traders.
8. University of Cambridge "'Gut Feelings.'"
9. Bottemanne, H., O. Morlaàs, P. Fossati, and L. Schmidt, L., "Does the Coronavirus Epidemic Take Advantage of Human Optimism Bias?," *Frontiers in Psychology* 11, no. 2001 (2020).
10. VanderPal, G., and R. Brazie, "Influence of Basic Human Behaviors (Influenced by Brain Architecture and Function), and Past Traumatic Events on Investor Behavior and Financial Bias," *Journal of Accounting and Finance* 22, no. 2 (2022): 14.
11. Daniel, K., and D. Hirshleifer, "Overconfident Investors, Predictable Returns, and Excessive Trading," *Journal of Economic Perspectives* 29, no. 4 (2015): 61–88.
12. Daniel and Hirshleifer, "Overconfident Investors."
13. VanderPal and Brazie, "Influence of Basic Human Behaviors," 14.
14. VanderPal and Brazie, "Influence of Basic Human Behaviors," 14.
15. Heryanda, K. K., "The Effect of Job Insecurity on Turnover Intention Through Work Satisfaction in Employees of Pt. Telkom Access Singaraja," *International Journal of Social Science and Business* 3, no. 3 (2019): 198–205.
16. Parcia, R. O., and E. T. Estimo, "Employees' Financial Literacy, Behavior, Stress and Wellness," *Journal of Human Resource Management* 5, no. 5 (2017): 78–89.
17. Parcia and Estimo, "Employees' Financial Literacy."
18. Bellucci, D., G. Fuochi, and P. Conzo, "Childhood Exposure to the Second World War and Financial Risk Taking in Adult Life," *Journal of Economic Psychology* 79 (2020): 102196.
19. Sullivan, R. N., "Deploying Financial Emotional Intelligence," *Financial Analysts Journal* 67, no. 6 (2011): 4–10.
20. Sullivan, "Deploying Financial Emotional Intelligence."

21. Somatic Experiencing International, "Transforming Lives Through Healing Trauma," https://traumahealing.org/.
22. Somatic Experiencing International, "Transforming Lives Through Healing Trauma."

CHAPTER 5
1. Bell, S. T., et al., "Team Composition and the ABCs of Teamwork," *American Psychologist* 73, no. 4 (2018): 349.
2. Bell et al., "Team Composition," 349.
3. Tasca, G. A., "Team Cognition and Reflective Functioning: A Review and Search for Synergy," *Group Dynamics: Theory, Research, and Practice* 25, no. 3 (2021): 258.
4. Tasca, "Team Cognition," 258.
5. Friedrich, T. L., J. A. Griffith, and M. D. Mumford, "Collective Leadership Behaviors: Evaluating the Leader, Team Network, and Problem Situation Characteristics That Influence Their Use," *The Leadership Quarterly* 27, 2 (2016): 312–333.
6. Seijts, G. H., and J. Gandz, "Transformational Change and Leader Character," *Business Horizons* 61, no. 2 (2017): 239–249.
7. Bell et al., "Team Composition," 349.
8. Bell et al., "Team Composition," 349.
9. Bisbey, T., and E. Salas, "Team Dynamics and Processes in the Workplace," in *Oxford Research Encyclopedia of Psychology* (United Kingdom: Oxford University Press, 2019).
10. Dana, Deb, *Polyvagal Exercises for Safety and Connection: 50 Client-Centered Practices* (New York: W. W. Norton & Company, 2020).
11. Dana, *Polyvagal Exercises.*
12. Dana, *Polyvagal Exercises.*
13. Bajwa, N. M., et al., "Intra Versus Interprofessional Conflicts: Implications for Conflict Management Training," *Journal of Interprofessional Care* 34, 2 (2020): 259–268.
14. Lacerenza, Christina N., et al., "Team Development Interventions: Evidence-Based Approaches for Improving Teamwork," *American Psychologist* 73, no. 4 (2018): 517.
15. Overton, A. R., and A. C. Lowry, "Conflict Management: Difficult Conversations with Difficult People," *Clinics in Colon and Rectal Surgery* 26, no. 4 (Dec 2013): 259–264, doi:10.1055/s-0033-1356728.
16. Gallo, A., *HBR Guide to Dealing with Conflict* (Boston: MA: Harvard Business Review Press, 2017), Kindle.

17. Williams, H. W., "Safety: Take a Threefold Approach to Create an Inclusive Workplace," *Opflow* 47, no. 10 (2021): 22–24.

18. Berry, D., and M. P. Bell, "Inequality in Organizations: Stereotyping, Discrimination, and Labor Law Exclusions," *Equality, Diversity and Inclusion: An International Journal* 31, no. 3 (2012).

19. Subhakaran, S. E., and Dyaram, L., "Interpersonal Antecedents to Employee Upward Voice: Mediating Role of Psychological Safety," *International Journal of Productivity and Performance Management* (2018).

20. Parcia, R. O., and E. T. Estimo, "Employees' Financial Literacy, Behavior, Stress and Wellness," *Journal of Human Resource Management* 5, no. 5 (2017): 78–89.

21. Volevakha, I. B., N. V. Kolomiiets, and T. V. Kukhar, "Organizational Factors of Psychological Safety in the Workplace," *Wiad Lek* 74, no. 11 (2021): 2789–2793.

22. Volevakha, Kolomiiets, and Kukhar, "Organizational Factors."

23. Dana, *Polyvagal Exercises.*

CHAPTER 6

1. Turner, A., "How Does Intrinsic and Extrinsic Motivation Drive Performance Culture in Organizations?," *Cogent Education* 4, no. 1 (2017): 1337543.

2. Kuvaas, B., R. Buch, A. Weibel, A. Dysvik, and C. G. Nerstad, "Do Intrinsic and Extrinsic Motivation Relate Differently to Employee Outcomes?," *Journal of Economic Psychology* 61 (2017): 246.

3. Turner, "Intrinsic and Extrinsic Motivation."

4. Ali, B. J., and G. Anwar, "An Empirical Study of Employees' Motivation and Its Influence Job Satisfaction," *International Journal of Engineering, Business and Management* 5, no. 2 (2021): 21–30.

5. Ali and Anwar, "An Empirical Study of Employees' Motivation."

6. Alam, F., L. Yifei, M. Raza, and K. Khan, "The Impact of Leader's Emotional Intelligence on Employee Organizational Behavior: Mediating Role of Employee Motivation," *European Academic Research* 6, no. 10 (2020): 5127–5154.

7. Trivedi, A. J., and A. Mehta, "Maslow's Hierarchy of Needs—Theory of Human Motivation," *International Journal of Research in all Subjects in Multi Languages* 7, no. 6 (2019); 38–41.

8. Lussier, K., "Of Maslow, Motives, and Managers: The Hierarchy of Needs in American Business, 1960–1985," *Journal of the History of the Behavioral Sciences* 55, no. 4 (2019): 319–341.

9. Lussier, "Of Maslow."

10. Taormina, R. J., and J. H. Gao, "Maslow and the Motivation Hierarchy: Measuring Satisfaction of the Needs," *The American Journal of Psychology* 126, no. 2 (2013): 155–177.

11. Bisbey, T., and E. Salas, "Team Dynamics and Processes in the Workplace," in *Oxford Research Encyclopedia of Psychology* (Oxford University Press, 2019).

12. Bisbey and Salas, "Team Dynamics."

13. Bisbey and Salas, "Team Dynamics."

14. Saud, T. R., "The Effect of Job Characteristics on Organizational Commitment: The Role of Growth Need Strength in Nepali IT Companies," *Journal of Business and Management Research* 3, no. 1–2 (2020): 39–56.

15. Mayrowetz, D., et al., "Distributed Leadership as Work Redesign: Retrofitting the Job Characteristics Model," *Leadership and Policy in Schools* 6, no. 1 (2007): 69–101.

16. Anjum, Z., et al., "Job Characteristics Model and Job Satisfaction," *International Journal of Education and Research* 2, no. 11 (2014): 241–262.

17. Anjum et al., "Job Characteristics Model."

18. Steyn, R., and N. Vawda, "Job Characteristics: Their Relationship to Job Satisfaction, Stress and Depression," *Journal of Psychology in Africa* 24, no. 3 (2014): 281–284.

19. Daniel, K., and D. Hirshleifer, "Overconfident Investors, Predictable Returns, and Excessive Trading," *Journal of Economic Perspectives* 29, no. 4 (2015): 61–88.

20. Paais, M., and J. R. Pattiruhu, "Effect of Motivation, Leadership, and Organizational Culture on Satisfaction and Employee Performance," *The Journal of Asian Finance, Economics and Business* 7, no. 8 (2020): 577–588.

21. Paais and Pattiruhu, "Effect of Motivation."

22. Al-Suraihi, W. A., et al., "Employee Turnover: Causes, Importance and Retention Strategies," *European Journal of Business and Management Research* 6, no. 3: 1–10.

23. Parcia, R. O., and E. T. Estimo, "Employees' Financial Literacy, Behavior, Stress and Wellness," *Journal of Human Resource Management* 5, no. 5 (2017): 78–89.

24. Men, L. R., Y. S. Qin, and J. Jin, "Fostering Employee Trust via Effective Supervisory Communication During the COVID-19 Pandemic: Through the Lens of Motivating Language Theory,"

International Journal of Business Communication 59, no. 2 (2017): 193–218.

25. Volevakha, I. B., N. V. Kolomiiets, and T. V. Kukhar, "Organizational Factors of Psychological Safety in the Workplace," *Wiad Lek* 74, no. 11 (2021): 2789–2793.
26. Turner, "Intrinsic and Extrinsic Motivation."
27. Turner, "Intrinsic and Extrinsic Motivation."
28. Turner, "Intrinsic and Extrinsic Motivation."
29. Kuvaas, B., R. Buch, A. Weibel, A. Dysvik, and C. G. Nerstad, "Do Intrinsic and Extrinsic Motivation Relate Differently to Employee Outcomes?," *Journal of Economic Psychology* 61 (2017): 246.
30. Dana, D., *Polyvagal Exercises for Safety and Connection: 50 Client-Centered Practices* (New York: W. W. Norton & Company, 2020).
31. Ali and Anwar, "An Empirical Study of Employees' Motivation."
32. Groysberg, B., et al., "The Leader's Guide to Corporate Culture," *Harvard Business Review* 96, no. 1 (2018): 44–52.
33. McKinnon, R. C., *Changing the Workplace Safety Culture* (Boca Raton, Florida: CRC Press, 2013), 43.

CHAPTER 7

1. Shah, B., "Effective Leadership in Organization," *European Journal of Business and Management Research* 3, no. 3 (2018): 1–5.
2. Shah, "Effective Leadership."
3. Bacon, B., "Intuitive Intelligence in Leadership," *Management Services* 57, no. 3 (2013), 26–29.
4. Bacon, "Intuitive Intelligence."
5. Bacon, "Intuitive Intelligence."
6. Porges, S. W., and Deb D., *Clinical Applications of the Polyvagal Theory: The Emergence of Polyvagal-Informed Therapies*, Norton Series on Interpersonal Neurobiology (New York: WW Norton & Company, 2018).
7. Slonim, T., "The Polyvagal Theory: Neuropsychological Foundations of Emotions, Attachment, Communication, and Self-Regulation," *International Journal of Group Psychotherapy* 64, no. 4 (2014): 593–600.
8. Slonim, "The Polyvagal Theory."
9. Flores, P. J., and S. W. Porges, "Group Psychotherapy as a Neural Exercise: Bridging Polyvagal Theory and Attachment Theory," *International Journal of Group Psychotherapy* 67, no. 2 (2017): 202–222.

10. Dana, D., *Polyvagal Exercises for Safety and Connection: 50 Client-Centered Practices* (New York: W. W. Norton & Company, 2020).

11. Dana, *Polyvagal Exercises.*

12. Dana, *Polyvagal Exercises.*

13. Dana, *Polyvagal Exercises.*

14. Porges, S. W., *The Polyvagal Theory: Neurophysiological Foundations of Emotions, Attachment, Communication, and Self-Regulation* (New York: W. W. Norton & Company, 2011), 230.

15. Porges, *The Polyvagal Theory*, 230.

16. Brown, R. P., and P. L. Gerbarg, "Breathing Techniques in Psychiatric Treatment," in *Complementary and Integrative Treatments in Psychiatric Practice*, eds. P. L. Gerbarg, P. R. Muskin, and R. P. Brown (Washington, D.C.: American Psychiatric Pub., 2017), 241–250.

17. Brown and Gerbarg, "Breathing Techniques."

18. Dana, *Polyvagal Exercises.*

19. Ghafur, R. D., G. Suri, and J. J. Gross, "Emotion Regulation Choice: The Role of Orienting Attention and Action Readiness," *Current Opinion in Behavioral Sciences* 19 (2018): 31–35.

20. Ghafur, Suri, and Gross, "Emotion Regulation Choice," 31.

21. Porges, *The Polyvagal Theory*, 230.

22. Porges, S. W. (2022). Polyvagal Theory: A Science of Safety. *Frontiers in Integrative Neuroscience*, 16.

23. Dana, *Polyvagal Exercises.*

24. Flores and Porges, "Group Psychotherapy as a Neural Exercise," 202–222.

25. Porges, S. W., "Polyvagal Theory: A Primer," *Clinical Applications of the Polyvagal Theory: The Emergence of Polyvagal-Informed Therapies* 50 (2018): 69.

26. Savavibool, N., B. Gatersleben, and C. Moorapun, "The Effects of Colour in Work Environment: A Systematic Review," *Asian Journal of Behavioural Studies* 3, no. 13 (2018): 149.

27. Pachito, D. V., et al., "Workplace Lighting for Improving Alertness and Mood in Daytime Workers," *Cochrane Database of Systematic Reviews*, 3 (2018).

28. Pachito et al., "Workplace Lighting."

29. Pachito et al., "Workplace Lighting."

30. Colenberg, S., T. Jylhä, and M. Arkesteijn, "The Relationship Between Interior Office Space and Employee Health and Well-Being—a Literature Review," *Building Research & Information* 49, 3 (2018): 352–366.

31. Lee, M. S., et al., "Interaction with Indoor Plants May Reduce Psychological and Physiological Stress by Suppressing Autonomic Nervous System Activity in Young Adults: A Randomized Crossover Study," *Journal of Physiological Anthropology* 34, no. 1 (2015): 1–6.

32. Jafari, M. J., et al., "The Effect of Noise Exposure on Cognitive Performance and Brain Activity Patterns," *Open Access Macedonian Journal of Medical Sciences* 7, no. 17 (2019): 2924.

33. Haley Bennett, "What Are White, Pink and Brown Noise," *BBC Science Focus*, February 25, 2023.

INDEX

ABOUT THE AUTHORS

Dr. Randy Brazie, MD, SEP®, is the former chief medical officer for Resilient Health, an Arizona nonprofit healthcare provider of innovative multimodal services for both public and private sectors. He currently serves as a medical director for Blue Cross Blue Shield of Arizona and has a private practice. He is board certified by the American Board of Psychiatry and Neurology in General Psychiatry and a Somatic Experiencing Practitioner. Dr. Brazie has extensive experience in multiple sectors, including both clinic and hospital-based services, as well as emergency and urgent care settings.

Dr. Geoffrey VanderPal, DBA, Certified Financial Planner™, Project Management Professional, Society of Human Resource Managers Senior Certified Professional, is a professor in the Master of Science in Finance program at Purdue University Global, where he teaches financial planning–related courses. He has taught at various universities on four continents in the areas of finance, leadership, and business. He also spent over 20 years as an entrepreneur founding several successful businesses and leading teams. Dr. VanderPal is the author of *Invincible Investing* and several dozen peer-reviewed research articles.